Praise for *The Complete Lea*

Jackie Beere's books are always worth reading. She has an eye for what works in classrooms and provides practical examples for busy teachers tackling tricky interdisciplinary issues outside their subject expertise. *The Complete Learner's Toolkit* is a veritable cornucopia of ideas for lessons – and any school wanting to enrich their PSHE offer or tutorial programme will want at least one copy in their staff library.

Sir Tim Brighouse, former London Schools Commissioner and
Chief Education Officer for Birmingham and Oxfordshire

This welcome book is another sign of the rapidly changing view as to the nature of learning and the focus on the skills and strategies needed by learners. Jackie Beere has produced a detailed, exhaustive and authoritative guide that combines a clear overview of the topic alongside supportive activities and case studies. Most importantly, the resources in this text provide a bridge between principle and practice.

The Complete Learner's Toolkit is to be welcomed because it goes into the detail that is so often missing, and it will give teachers and learners the confidence to apply the ideas and develop alternative ways of thinking and working.

John West-Burnham, Honorary Professor, University of Worcester

The Complete Learner's Toolkit is a vital resource for effectively equipping the modern learner with the 21st century skills required to succeed and thrive in our fast-changing world. This insightful toolkit is essential for school leaders, teachers and parents to help them provide children and young people with the very best possible education and start in life.

Justin Blake, UK Country Lead, HundrED, and education consultant

The Complete Learner's Toolkit outlines lessons to develop the language of, and strategies for, learning, and focuses on the most important aspect of learning: teaching students to become their own teachers. Surely, if lifelong learning is to be realised, being able to teach oneself is essential. This entails knowing when and where to get help from an expert, how to evaluate the myriad of information now available, knowing how to prioritise, and using evaluative thinking in order to determine where to go next in the learning journey.

John Hattie, Laureate Professor, Melbourne Graduate School of Education,
University of Melbourne

In recent decades we have learned an awful lot about how learning happens through a focus on ideas such as mindset, memory and metacognition. Generally, these ideas are talked about – and fiercely debated over – among adults. In *The Complete*

Learner's Toolkit, Jackie Beere has created a treasure trove of activities that bring these ideas to life in a way that children can get to grips with – all rooted in an expansive vision of education that stretches beyond employability skills and into the realms of self-regulated learning and self-actualisation.

As we edge inevitably into an age characterised by algorithms, AI and autonomous vehicles, I am sure *The Complete Learner's Toolkit* will be of great use to teachers, parents and young people themselves for many years to come.

Dr James Mannion, Bespoke Programmes Leader, UCL Institute of Education, and
co-author of *Fear is the Mind Killer: Why Learning to Learn Deserves Lesson Time
– and How to Make It Work for Your Pupils*

The Complete Learner's Toolkit is an essential book for every school because it provides lessons for children that will help them be more resilient, become more motivated learners, and improve their skills in readiness for working life.

As a school governor with decades of experience in business, I welcome this exciting package of ideas that will help the next generation thrive in an even more demanding work environment. For school leaders and teachers, Jackie Beere's book provides a crucial addition to the curriculum offer so that they can support and develop the essential skills for wellbeing, collaboration and rising to the challenges of 21st century life.

Gill Watton, Vice Chair of School Governors, the Elmwood and Penrose Federation

In *The Complete Learner's Toolkit* Jackie writes and shares from first-hand experience of what really matters and what should be at the heart of all outstanding classrooms. Addressing the needs of teachers and students alike, it will equip everyone who reads it with the intrinsic tools to make lifelong learning a success.

In addition, the book is a valuable CPD guide to help teachers of all levels of experience model positive attitudes and behaviours so that their students can excel and emerge from school with a skill set that will set them up for lifelong success. Jackie offers a multitude of practical advice and easy-to-follow lessons, all crafted to sit alongside the skills identified by the World Economic Forum. Emotional intelligence (EQ), growth mindset and metacognitive strategies are the irrefutable pillars of the book's content, all made so easy for practitioners to access through these well-designed resources.

Overall, *The Complete Learner's Toolkit* is a great addition to any teaching and learning library, and a resource that will surely stand the test of time.

Helen Boyle, Advanced Skills Teacher, Teacher of Religious Studies/Humanities,
St Christopher's School, Bahrain

The world is changing and, if we're to solve the problems facing our planet, schools must change too. *The Complete Learner's Toolkit* is the essential companion for teachers and school leaders who are ambitious about a better future for humanity.

Getting good grades is no longer enough; metacognition, mindset and character are essential in developing a purposeful disposition to the world. The ideas set out in this book are infused with the shrewd wisdom born out of Jackie Beere's extensive school experience. Not only do the book's activities help teachers to foster essential and in-demand workplace skills in children, they also make them more confident, empathetic and creative citizens. Being creative means breaking the rules – and finding solutions to complex problems, such as catastrophic global climate change, pandemic control and extreme poverty and violence, requires expert problem solvers.

The Complete Learner's Toolkit gives children the confidence to lead, the adaptability to learn and the values and generosity of spirit to make good choices and sensible decisions in life. This book is about no less than human flourishing and encourages every teacher and school leader to harness the enormous power of the next generation on a now-fragile planet and in an increasingly unequal world.

Ian Loynd, Head Teacher, St Teilo's Church in Wales High School

The Complete
Learner's
Toolkit

Metacognition and mindset – equipping the modern
learner with the thinking, social and self-regulation
skills to succeed at school and in life

Jackie Beere

independent
thinking press

First published by

Independent Thinking Press, Crown Buildings, Bancyfelin, Carmarthen, Wales, SA33 5ND, UK

and

Independent Thinking Press, PO Box 2223, Williston, VT 05495, USA

www.independentthinkingpress.com

Independent Thinking Press is an imprint of Crown House Publishing Ltd.

British Library Cataloguing-in-Publication Data

A catalogue entry for this book is available from the British Library.

Print ISBN 978-178135317-2
Mobi ISBN 978-178135366-0
ePub ISBN 978-178135367-7
ePDF ISBN 978-178135368-4

LCCN 2020931170

Printed and bound in the UK by
Gomer Press, Llandysul, Ceredigion

For all the heroes of the NHS and other key workers who served the country so fearlessly during the 2020 pandemic. They are our role models.

Foreword

Like all head teachers, I am always searching for resources that will equip our teachers to deliver the best possible learning experiences to our students. *The Complete Learner's Toolkit* does exactly that, while delivering so much more.

I have had the pleasure of working with Jackie Beere, as we are both Associates of Independent Thinking. I have always admired her philosophy in relation to teaching and learning over the years – that is, putting the students at the heart of teachers' planning, thus responding to their emotional and social needs, which also has a positive impact on their academic achievements.

Jackie is an educator who passionately believes in students developing a growth mindset and a self-belief in themselves as learners. In this book she draws upon the current research available around growth mindset, resilience and communication – and, in a rapidly changing world, these are essential for students to have in order to develop their workplace skills.

As a school that puts values-based education at the heart of its work, the outcomes we desire for our students are centred around the values of respect, responsibility and resilience. Using *The Complete Learner's Toolkit* will enable our teachers to fully explore with students what resilience is and how to develop it as they grow. Each of the lessons builds these skills and enables students to develop a deeper understanding of self and of how to apply their new learning – helping them to thrive and not just survive.

Respect from others emerges once students understand how to respect themselves. The activities in this book are planned to enable students to understand themselves and their relationships with their peers, and to explore the most effective ways in which to learn. Ultimately, we are all responsible for the decisions we make and we want our students to choose what they know is right for them in the different contexts they find themselves. *The Complete Learner's Toolkit* makes students consider ways in which they can build the courage to take necessary risks and be responsible for those choices.

Schools that explicitly teach students to develop a growth mindset reap the rewards when students are faced with challenging situations academically and are able to demonstrate that they can persevere. It also raises achievement in the classroom as students' critical thinking and problem-solving skills improve. *The Complete Learner's Toolkit* takes this understanding even deeper when it teaches students about their amazing brain. To have some basic understanding of the neuroscience that underpins how we work as humans is powerful for students – and to be able to 'identify parts of the brain', talk about 'neural pathways' with their peers and discuss the work of Piaget, Pavlov and Dweck empowers students to deepen their understanding using accessible language.

Students are naturally curious. By asking the kinds of enquiry questions that feature throughout *The Complete Learner's Toolkit*, it reinforces the idea that asking questions is a strength – and we, as teachers, should be encouraging our students to remain curious about the world they are growing up in. It also empowers pupils to ask such questions when they may feel pressurised by their peers: 'What are we doing?' 'What impact are we having on our community?' 'How will this make us better people?'

If there was one thing I would give as a gift to all students, it would be confidence. So many students are influenced by external pressures, especially through social media. *The Complete Learner's Toolkit* focuses on students gaining an understanding of their emotional intelligence – which, in turn, encompasses self-awareness and self-management skills and, in doing so, builds tolerance and confidence. These are fundamental attributes that can empower students to become the leaders of the future. Everyone is a leader in their own right, and to own confidence in self while understanding and trusting others forms the basis of excellent relationships.

Ultimately, *The Complete Learner's Toolkit* will help shape students' attitudes towards themselves and provide them with a better understanding of how they learn. If the tools and lessons contained within this book are shared effectively and with compassion, then the students of today will be well equipped to make the world of tomorrow a better place to be.

Julie Rees, Head Teacher of Ledbury Primary School

Acknowledgements

In my long career in education I have worked as a teacher, school leader and trainer. I must thank the thousands of children, teachers and colleagues I have met along the way. They have inspired me and reinforced my realisation that passing on the skills and attributes covered in this book will make a difference to our children. I particularly want to thank the inspiring and aspiring school leaders who put children at the centre of their mission and who know that teachers have the power to make a difference and are brave enough to give them a chance to do so.

I would like to thank all the staff at Crown House Publishing and Independent Thinking Press, who have been so patient and supportive through the development of this book. From Ian, who inspired me with ideas to reinvent this toolkit, to Louise who trawled through the copy so many times to help improve the content. A very special thank you also goes to Mandy Fry for spending so much time creating the illustrations and responding to my endless requests.

Most of all I would like to thank my wonderful family: Mum, Di, Les and Rob, who are always there for encouragement and support; my three inspiring daughters – Lucy, Kirstie and Carrie – and the pure joy of my grandkids, who remind me every day that the future is theirs.

Finally, I want to say a huge thank you to my husband, John, who is 'simply the best'. He has supported, critiqued, edited and simply given me all the love I need to do what I do.

Contents

Introduction:

Why this book is essential for our children

We know that schools have a much more important job to do than simply prepare children for exams. This book adds personal development to your curriculum in a powerful and exciting way. It contains 36 lessons which have been devised around the World Economic Forum's projections of essential and in-demand workplace skills for the 2020s.[1] Teaching these skills is necessary if our children are to grow up with the resilience, confidence and communication skills that will help them to thrive in an ever-changing world and workplace. Research shows us that socio-emotional skills have declined in the last 30 years, especially for boys.[2] Further research shows us that children who are taught these skills as part of the curriculum or as discrete courses show improved behaviour and attainment:

Treated children become less impulsive, less disruptive, and display less opposition to teachers and parents. In class, treated children become less likely to disturb lessons and more likely to focus on the teaching content.[3]

Each lesson in this book can be used as a stand-alone or incorporated into a topic or subject context. The lessons encourage the habits of reflection and metacognition that give children the power to manage their thinking. They also include many practical strategies that will help them maximise their learning potential and improve self-regulation.

1   A. Gray, The 10 Skills You Need to Thrive in the Fourth Industrial Revolution, *World Economic Forum* (19 January 2016). Available at: https://www.weforum.org/agenda/2016/01/the-10-skills-you-need-to-thrive-in-the-fourth-industrial-revolution/.
2   O. Attanasio, R. Blundell, G. Conti and G. Mason, *Inequality in Socioemotional Skills: A Cross-Cohort Comparison.* IFS Working Paper W18/22 (London: Institute for Fiscal Studies, 2018), p. 1. Available at: https://www.ifs.org.uk/uploads/publications/wps/WP201822.pdf.
3   G. Sorrenti, U. Zölitz, D. Ribeaud and M. Eisner, *The Causal Impact of Socio-Emotional Skills Training on Educational Success.* IZA Discussion Paper No. 13087 (March 2020), p. 47. Available at: https://papers.ssrn.com/sol3/papers.cfm?abstract_id=3562877.

The context for teaching these skills

New tasks at work are driving a demand for essential skills that are not always a focus in the curriculum.

The world is changing. The skills required to perform most jobs are constantly evolving, as reflected in the World Economic Forum's ever-shifting projections of necessary workplace skills. They have gone through several updates, even as I have been working on this book. I remain confident, however, that the skills targeted in these lessons will be of use to children throughout their lives – in the classroom and beyond it in the world of work and in their daily lives. In three decades of teaching students and teachers, I've seen how the skills identified here have had the most powerful impact on developing outstanding learners. I have witnessed this in students, teachers, myself and my own children. These lessons aim to develop the social skills essential for students to work together in groups and allow them to tap into the synergy found in collaborative learning.

Rapid technological advancement certainly has an influence, but proficiency in new technologies is only one part of the future skills equation. 'Human' skills such as creativity, originality, initiative, critical thinking, persuasion and negotiation are expected to increase in value, as is attention to detail, resilience, flexibility and complex problem solving. Emotional intelligence, leadership and social influence are also set to see a marked increase in importance.[4] Developing these skills will require learners to have confidence, high levels of self-awareness and a mindset that relishes challenge. These skills are most powerful when taught in the context of the knowledge domain so that they are transferred effectively in practical applications every day.

A lot of these lessons focus on how learners think about learning, and about themselves, informed by Carol Dweck's extensive research on growth mindset. She concludes that those who believe that they can grow their intelligence through struggle and effort make more progress.[5] However, the strategies around growth mindset don't provide a single 'magic bullet'. We are all a mixture of growth and fixed mindset, so it is vital to help our students know when to use growth mindset thinking to avoid giving up when facing a learning challenge.

---

4   V. S. Ratcheva and T. Leopold, 5 Things to Know About the Future of Jobs, *World Economic Forum* (17 September 2019). Available at: https://www.weforum.org/agenda/2018/09/future-of-jobs-2018-things-to-know/.

5   C. Dweck, *Mindset: The New Psychology of Success* (New York: Ballantine Books, 2006).

Jim Collins highlights the importance of having the 'right people' on the bus in a business context to make your enterprise a success.[6] He emphasises that being the right person has more to do with character traits than with knowledge or skills. With a growth mindset, we understand that such character traits are not set in stone but can be nurtured and developed.

Children (and adults) with a growth mindset believe that their basic qualities can be developed through dedication and hard work. They believe that struggle equals growth and that effort is the path to mastery. This view creates a love of learning and a resilience that I have seen is essential for lifelong success.

The activities in this book will help children become aware of how their thinking influences their mindset, so that change and growth in their emotional intelligence becomes possible. A growth mindset also affords us a level of emotional literacy that enables us to develop useful learning habits such as resilience and self-management. As children develop an acceptance of failure as an essential part of learning, they become the fearless learners they need to be in times of uncertainty.

Teaching about growth mindset – how and, particularly, *when* to use it – creates motivation and raises achievement in the classroom and the staffroom. It turns mistakes into learning experiences and it also enhances wellbeing and relationships. A growth mindset approach is fundamental to developing the skills which the World Economic Forum identifies as essential and on which this book focuses. These are:

- Active learning and learning strategies.
- Complex problem solving.
- Critical thinking.
- Creativity.
- Leadership and social influence.
- Emotional intelligence.
- Judgement and decision making.
- Service orientation.
- Negotiation.
- Cognitive flexibility.[7]

6 J. Collins, *Good to Great: Why Some Companies Make the Leap … and Others Don't* (London: Random House Business Books, 2001), p. 64.

7 This list is an amalgam of what I see as the most important skills from the World Economic Forum's most recent lists. See Gray, *The 10 Skills You Need to Thrive in the Fourth Industrial Revolution*; and Ratcheva and Leopold, *5 Things to Know About the Future of Jobs*.

The lessons in this book are for teachers to use with students aged 7–16 (Key Stages 2–4 in England) to help them become aware of their own strengths and personal challenges and give them an insight into how to develop these lifelong learning skills for themselves. This book can be used as a course for the whole class or dipped into when needed with groups or individuals. The bonus is that this resource will not only develop great thinking habits in the young people but also in ourselves. In teaching these lessons, we can learn so much!

Developing and embedding a learning culture

There is a continuing debate about whether we should teach the skills of how we learn in addition to the content of the curriculum. However, there is no such dispute about the importance of the quality of teaching, and teachers' mindsets, to school improvement. By using this book as an integral toolkit for developing outstanding learning, you can improve learning *and* teaching.

Including lessons on learning skills in the curriculum can help teachers to understand the barriers to learning that some children face. It helps children to develop more strategies for learning in every subject, and supports more independent learning in every lesson. As James Mannion and Kate McAllister discover in their book *Fear is the Mind Killer*, this is especially true for disadvantaged children:

there is an abundance of compelling research evidence to suggest that teaching pupils in ways that engage and develop metacognitive and self-regulatory processing leads to demonstrable, statistically significant gains across a range of pupil outcomes.[8]

In Sea View, one secondary school cited in the book, learning skills lessons were introduced as a complex intervention across the curriculum. Leaders prioritised a learning skills culture and teachers developed their own crucial skills of self-regulation, metacognition and oracy as part of the whole-school continuing professional

---

8   J. Mannion and K. McAllister, *Fear is the Mind Killer: Why Learning to Learn Deserves Lesson Time – and How to Make It Work for Your Pupils* (Woodbridge: John Catt Educational, 2020), p. 45.

development (CPD), which also helped them to model a learning mindset in their own classrooms.

If you are to deliver a bespoke learning skills curriculum that suits the context of your school, the leadership must back it. In my experience, as a head teacher leading a school which implemented this course, it must be a school-wide priority for the skills to penetrate every aspect of teaching and learning. All staff need to be trained in the skills and their purpose, but there must also be dedicated teachers to deliver discrete lessons in the skills. The teachers who deliver these lessons must not be conscripts but evangelists who have a passion for developing independent learners. This was also the conclusion in the Sea View experience:

if you really want your students to become effective, self-regulated learners, you need to provide them with dedicated lessons in which this work can take place.[9]

The exciting result of the Sea View project was to transform a school in special measures into one that closed the gap for pupil premium students more effectively than any other school in the region. There were also real gains in GCSE outcomes for all students who experienced learning skills lessons in Key Stage 3:

the results followed a very similar pattern to the interim results at the end of Year 9, with statistically significant gains in subject learning among the Learning Skills cohort as a whole, and among students from disadvantaged backgrounds (i.e., those eligible for the PP).[10]

To make the most of the material in this book and create the best outcomes for students, teachers should also treat these lessons as personal CPD. Doing so can help them to embed the skills and mindsets which this book promotes in their teaching, and so model them for their students. Teachers can also consider how best to adapt the lessons in this book and how to incorporate the World Economic Forum essential skills within their subject specialisms. In my own experience, teaching these skills to 11- to 14-year-olds made me a much more flexible and successful teacher, achieving outstanding examination results in my subject, and enabling me to become an advanced skills teacher (AST) and eventually a teacher trainer.

9   Mannion and McAllister, *Fear is the Mind Killer*, p. 112.
10 Mannion and McAllister, *Fear is the Mind Killer*, p. 254.

No doubt the debate around skills and knowledge will continue. However, I hope that this book will provide a useful resource that will help students – and teachers – to achieve their true potential.

A teachers' guide to understanding the skills developed in this book

Active learning and learning strategies

 Aim: To help students understand more about how their brains work so that they become more effective learners.

We know that learning changes brains. Learning grows new neural pathways, enabling us to develop new skills and solve problems. If we want our learners to retain new knowledge long term, they need to embed these neural pathways by applying the knowledge in novel situations, using it to problem-solve while enjoying the process. The terminal examinations that currently dominate many curricula require confident mastery and retention of the knowledge, not merely rote learning which is shallow and short term. It is essential that we teach our students how to review their learning, maximise their memory and grow their neural pathways so that they can perform in these examinations and – beyond them – be prepared and able to tackle new challenges.

One of the most important research discoveries about knowledge and memory, according to Peter Brown et al. in *Make It Stick*, is that active retrieval is the most powerful way to strengthen learning.[11] Making a determined effort to recall your knowledge and test yourself on it works. And the more challenging the test, the more beneficial the impact, so struggling to remember and working very hard at it really does grow your brainpower. By finding out more about how their brains work in these lessons, students will understand how important it is to persist in finding strategies that will increase their ability and potential.

---

11 P. Brown, H. Roediger and M. McDaniel, *Make It Stick: The Science of Successful Learning* (Cambridge, MA: Harvard University Press, 2014), p. 59.

When learning is harder, it's stronger and lasts longer.

Peter Brown et al.[12]

Discovering how their brains work will encourage our students to see that they need to use it or lose it! Research by Stanislas Dehaene, professor of experimental cognitive psychology at the Collège de France, suggests that a baby's brain is far from a blank slate: it is, in fact, a sophisticated structure with its own innate language of thought.[13] Education hones our abilities, and improvements in learning rely on attention, active engagement, error, feedback and sleep, among other things. These lessons encourage active learning and raise awareness of strategies that will help motivate students and stimulate brainpower. Dehaene suggests that 'no dyslexia or dyscalculia is so strong as to be beyond the reach of rehabilitation', because of the amazing power of brain plasticity.[14] This means we should never underestimate children's ability to learn. The most important message for our students is that we all have truly amazing brains – and that learning fuels our brainpower – so the harder we work, the smarter we become.

Metacognition – the ability to know oneself, to self-evaluate, to mentally simulate what would happen if we acted this way or that way – plays a fundamental role in human learning. The opinions we form of ourselves help us progress or, in some cases, lock us into a vicious circle of failure.

Stanislas Dehaene[15]

In addition, Part 1 will help you to help develop students' personal wellbeing by getting them to understand why they become emotional, frustrated, angry or excited. These lessons help students to develop metacognition as a habit that will create natural resilience. As John Hattie stresses, 'Resilience is the ability to react to adversity, challenge, tension, or failure in an adaptive and productive manner.'[16] It is an essential quality for learning and for life.

---

12 Brown, Roediger and McDaniel, *Make It Stick*, p. 9.

13 S. Dehaene, *How We Learn: The New Science of Education and the Brain* (London: Allen Lane, 2020), p. 82.

14 Dehaene, *How We Learn*, p. 82.

15 Dehaene, *How We Learn*, p. 22.

16 J. Hattie, *Visible Learning for Teachers: Maximizing Impact on Learning* (Abingdon and New York: Routledge, 2012), p. 59.

Complex problem solving

 Aim: To remind students that they are natural problem solvers and that there are many ways to tackle any problems they face in their learning.

According to Mike Berners-Lee, we have created an ever more complicated and complex world, demanding a challenging mix of interdependency and technical mastery.[17] However, we are born problem solvers. Children are experts at solving problems. As infants, they solved the problem of how to get fed, talk, walk and adapt to life. They did it through playing, watching, listening, copying, practising and learning how to learn, showing that we – as a species – are natural problem solvers who can follow our instincts to work out what to do next.

What gets in the way of this innate ability later in life is getting stuck in our own thinking. We begin to feel uncomfortable when we start to compare our performance with that of others – and judge ourselves against them – instead of staying in the moment. Frustration, confusion and mistakes are an important part of problem solving but they will stop us making progress if we see encountering them as evidence of our limitations or weaknesses, rather than as a source of information that will help us make progress. These lessons remind us that solving complex problems is an adventure that involves improvisation, experimentation, repetition, feedback and, again, that to struggle is to grow.

In the foreseeable future, humanity's challenges will include complex problems such as global warming, ocean acidification, mass migration, water shortages, nuclear proliferation, political instability, pandemic control, internet insecurity and an aging population (to name only a few!) – all of which will need to be tackled using a wealth of problem-solving skills.

---

17 M. Berners-Lee, *There Is No Planet B: A Handbook for the Make or Break Years* (Cambridge: Cambridge University Press, 2019), p. 189.

Critical thinking

 Aim: To help students realise and practise how to think and reflect objectively so that they can make good judgements.

Critical thinking is a crucial skill for achieving success at school and at work in later life. It involves observing, analysing, assessing and evaluating evidence in an objective, open-minded manner. It also asks that we cultivate a sense of curiosity that is always willing to ask questions. This skill will be developed in all the lessons in this book, but these particular lessons and activities in Part 3 will focus on sharpening children's abilities in this area, so that they can recognise and use this powerful tool for learning.

Socratic questioning is at the heart of critical thinking. Using open questions in the classroom and for homework helps deepen students' understanding and helps embed knowledge. In addition, developing the habit of critical thinking will help your students grow up to be open-minded and willing to listen to both sides of an argument before making up their minds. This could be a recipe for a less divided society!

In *There Is No Planet B*, Mike Berners-Lee concludes that we need to develop new thinking to ensure our survival on planet Earth. This includes global empathy, which means becoming more aware of our wider impact on others as our 'daily lives affect those on the other side of the world'.[18] Developing a critical thinking perspective will help our future citizens to stand back from their personal needs and consider the wider implications of their lifestyles.

It is crucially important for our students to be able to discern who and what to trust in our current world of fake news and self-curated imagery. Critical thinking will give them the ability to discern fact from fiction in an 'increasingly complex media and political sea of claim and counterclaim.'[19] If we can develop this skill in the next generation in schools, democracy stands more chance of being protected from corruption.

---

18 Berners-Lee, *There Is No Planet B*, p. 186.
19 Berners-Lee, *There Is No Planet B*, p. 189.

Creativity

Aim: To make students consider ways in which they can have the courage to take necessary risks to find new ways of thinking.

Creativity develops new thinking, leading to different approaches and novel ways of doing things, solving problems and finding new answers. It takes courage to be creative because as we grow older, we get used to doing things in ways that make us feel comfortable. We become creatures of habit, with the tendency to sit in the same places, read the same newspapers, listen to the same style of music and have similar friends with similar hobbies.

To step out of this comfort zone and become more creative involves taking a risk. Being creative means breaking the rules – innovating, finding new solutions and pushing back the boundaries. This takes courage and confidence as it could go wrong. These lessons encourage children to be brave and to create new experiences and new thinking – habitually.

If you don't embrace the fact that you think about the world in different ways, you severely limit your chances of finding the person that you were meant to be.

Ken Robinson[20]

Creativity can be a risky business: that's why it's linked to resilience. We all have our comfort zones, and they mould our behaviours until they become habits. Students also like to stay in their comfort zones, but we can help them get comfortable with pushing the boundaries. They need to work with a variety of different people, enjoy the challenges and opportunities presented by new experiences and new thinking. To do this, we may have to accept that we, as teachers, must be the creative role models, as Andrew Morrish suggests:

---

20 K. Robinson with L. Aronica, *The Element: How Finding Your Passion Changes Everything* (London: Penguin, 2009), p. 49.

As I have got older I've come to learn that, like most teachers, I am now one of the most creative people I know. More importantly, this also makes me one of the most influential people I know, because as a changemaker who has learnt to harness that creativity, I now have the power to innovate forever at my fingertips.[21]

Creativity demands risk-taking, and the inevitable failures that it incurs should be seen as part of the iterative process. Becoming comfortable with experimenting with novel ideas, taking feedback and redrafting work enables our innate childlike creativity to grow. Developing in our students the confidence to be as creative in their school lives as they were when they played happily as toddlers will insure them against personal stagnation and help ensure economic success for the enterprises and societies in which they work.

Leadership and social influence

 Aim: To help students develop the skills to lead and communicate effectively.

The skills needed to get on with other people are key to success at school and in the workplace. Good interpersonal relationships and the confidence to be a leader can be developed and nurtured in school. In these lessons we will explore strategies that can help children develop empathy, communication and leadership skills. These strategies can be built on in *every* lesson, as students work on their curriculum tasks in groups or pairs.

Students are massively influenced by their peers, especially as they get older. These lessons will help them understand how to lead, rather than to follow, and understand how to work in harmony with their peers. When you develop a classroom culture that combines challenge and nurture, where children unconditionally support each other's learning, as described by Carol Dweck, it develops the ultimate climate for good progress for all.[22]

---

21 A. Morrish, *The Art of Standing Out: School Transformation, to Greatness and Beyond* (Woodbridge: John Catt Educational, 2016), p. 178.
22 Dweck, *Mindset*, p. 198.

Emotional intelligence

 Aim: To help students develop the self-awareness and emotional regulation that will serve them well at school, at home and in their future workplace.

Emotional intelligence, or emotional quotient (EQ), encompasses self-awareness and self-management skills which develop confidence, tolerance and success.[23] Emotional intelligence combines interpersonal and intrapersonal intelligence and leads to the development of expert communication skills. Becoming emotionally intelligent helps children to see 'struggle' as 'growth' because they can stand back from their automatic negative response to struggling and enjoy a challenge without self-judgment or comparison with others. This habit of metacognition, or stepping back from your thinking, helps create that all-important growth mindset.

Emotional intelligence helps your students to manage their responses to the challenges of learning and of growing up. Employers value employees with high levels of emotional intelligence and this quality is set to remain an essential one, according to World Economic Forum predictions. Leadership training is often focused, for good reasons, on the development of thinking habits that encourage such self-awareness. These lessons will give your students a chance to understand the importance of EQ and how to grow this alongside their academic skills. For some children, school presents the only opportunity to develop the emotional intelligence that others may have the good fortune to have nurtured in their home environment. For happiness and wellbeing, as well as for success at school and in their careers, we must help our students to value and evolve their emotional intelligence.

Judgement and decision making

 Aim: To help students identify their values and encourage them to make conscious choices for their own benefit.

---

23 D. Goleman, *Emotional Intelligence: Why It Can Matter More Than IQ* (London: Bloomsbury, 1996).

Having good judgement and being able to make sensible decisions is an essential skill for us all. So why is it that some children (and, indeed, some adults) make choices that endanger their health and happiness? These lessons help students to think purposefully about their personal values and how they can use them to make good choices and sensible decisions in life. When children become susceptible to peer pressure, it is often because they haven't yet developed a clear set of their own values, which can act as an anchor in their tough formative years. The other purpose of these lessons is for students to practise standing back from their immediate, often automatic, responses and to think through the consequences of their decisions, so that they get in the habit of making good judgements.

In *The Chimp Paradox*, psychiatrist Steve Peters – who coached the Great Britain Cycling Team and the snooker player Ronnie O'Sullivan to perform at their best using his mind management programme – talks of 'the Stone of Life'.[24] This is a method of clarifying your beliefs and values so that you can draw on them in moments of crisis. Peters suggests that we all have a set of beliefs we hold to be true and that these influence our responses to events. This provokes a cognitive bias that can work unconsciously on our thoughts and feelings. For example, if you believe 'struggle is growth', you will be able to cope with failure better than if you believe 'struggle is inadequacy'. He suggests that it is useful to clarify helpful values and beliefs to guide wise decisions.

The mind management metaphor alluded to in the title of his book suggests that the emotional brain acts like a chimp on our shoulder, which can whisper in our ears and disempower us with self-doubt and anxiety. He suggests that the secret to health and happiness is to learn to 'manage' the chimp and 'harness its strength and power'.[25] The chimp is hugely creative; it can imagine monsters as well as amazing ideas and solutions. Helping students to clarify their values and showing them how this can provide them with confidence when making choices is so essential that it should be every student's entitlement.

---

24 S. Peters, *The Chimp Paradox: The Mind Management Programme to Help You Achieve Success, Confidence and Happiness* (London: Vermilion, 2012), p. 82.

25 Peters, *The Chimp Paradox*, p. 4.

Service orientation

Aim: To encourage students to want to help other people and to take pride in delivering high-quality outcomes.

The idea of being 'in service' could be seen as demeaning – perhaps slightly reminiscent of domestic duties or outmoded class hierarchies. However, adopting the mindset of serving others is a very powerful way to see the emergence of a generous spirit and the humility of true self-confidence. When we genuinely want others to be happy and satisfied with how we treat them and take pride in our work, whether we are leaders or not, we learn the dignity and self-esteem that can lead to our own peace and happiness. Helping children to understand how 'helping others helps me' will also build the thinking habits that will enable them to reap the rewards of learning from others in our diverse society, in which there are so many different perspectives.

Having a service orientation basically means actively looking for ways to help others, and it is contingent on utilising social skills. When adopting this outlook, there is a natural inclination to deliver high standards and to work hard to do the very best job possible. Ron Berger describes how nurturing a desire to deliver excellence can transform students' confidence and motivation when they create real-life projects that serve a purpose in the world.[26] This also creates a desire to seek out feedback – to improve and to maintain a courageous spirit of enterprise – helping students to improve their work ethic at school and, later, at work.

Negotiation

Aim: To practise good listening and communication skills that will empower students to develop healthy relationships.

Being able to negotiate involves effective communication and emotional resilience. To be able to stand back from your emotions so that you can take an objective view and see all aspects of a situation also requires metacognition and a growth mindset –

---

26 R. Berger, *An Ethic of Excellence: Building a Culture of Craftsmanship with Students* (Portsmouth, NH: Heinemann, 2003).

qualities that these lessons will nurture. These lessons will also develop the gifts of patient listening and empathy that make great negotiators.

There is another reason why empathy is an important habit for negotiation: empathetic people are great at getting rapport. Getting rapport elicits wonderful states of cooperation and motivation and means that others can connect with you, which, in turn, enhances your negotiation skills and ability to be a powerful communicator. Teachers who have high levels of empathy can get kids on side and spread the culture of compassion that is an essential underpinning of an 'outstanding' school community. Those children who struggle to show empathy may find it harder to understand the impact of any bad behaviour and, as a result, be more likely to commit crimes.

These lessons will help those children who find it hard to understand others' perspectives to deliberately develop the habit of empathy. This starts with a deliberate focus on listening with a clear mind. We can't hear others if we are too full of our own thoughts and concerns. Mindfulness practice helps us all understand how to clear our minds, and regular practice to enhance wellbeing is recommended within a school setting – as well as within these lessons.

Cognitive flexibility

Aim: To help students to be adaptable in new situations and to maximise their learning capacity.

Cognitive flexibility is the ability to change your mind and adapt to different circumstances. This will create resilience and confidence and, above all, a growth mindset that deals effectively with change.

[Our] unique human ability [is] to be able to turn our thoughts inwards and observe ourselves and our own mental life. This is an extraordinarily powerful observation because it is only through this ability that you can understand your own emotions and hence the emotions of others.

Andrew Curran[27]

27 A. Curran, *The Little Book of Big Stuff About the Brain: The True Story of Your Amazing Brain* (Carmarthen: Crown House Publishing, 2008), p. 22.

Our own individual day-to-day experiences of life are influenced by our conscious and unconscious thinking habits. We all sometimes suffer from cognitive biases: those sets of fixed beliefs about the way things are, or about our own attributes. For example, students may believe that they are poor learners or that maths is too difficult for them, that making friends is too hard or that singing in tune is too tricky. These beliefs may have been triggered by comments or comparisons with others, but once formed they can be hard to challenge. For example, if your ego is convinced that you can't spell, it will always look for evidence that it is right about that. So, when you struggle with a word, it runs the mental commentary, 'See, I can't spell – I have never been able to spell.'

This type of fixed thinking can apply to any aspect of life, from 'My relationships never work' to 'I can't do technology'. The more inflexible our thinking becomes, the more we are stuck believing that we can never change – not a useful state for learning!

> Your ego is simply your thinking about yourself. It is mostly invisible, habitual and running in the background all the time.
>
> Ken Manning et al.[28]

Our minds are always processing a myriad of random thoughts at any one time – if our habitual, default thinking is negative and self-doubting, then we will focus on the thoughts that fit with this perception and connect them together to create negative, sad or hopeless feelings. By noticing our feelings and becoming conscious of the thinking that is shaping them we become more self-reflective, slowing down our automatic emotional responses. We are then no longer being 'driven blindly' or trying to cling to past cognitive habits that don't serve us well. This quality is emphasised by Mike Berners-Lee as a key new way of thinking which is required for the 21st century.[29]

---

28 K. Manning, R. Charbit and S. Krot, *Invisible Power: Insight Principles at Work* (Lexington, MA: Insight Principles Inc., 2015), p. 148.
29 Berners-Lee, *There Is No Planet B*, p. 188.

> We have seen [...] how urgently we need to learn how to think in ways that let us deal more effectively with the situation we have created for ourselves. We need thinking skills and habits that fit in the twenty-first century context of enormous human power and technology on a now-fragile planet.
>
> Mike Berners-Lee[30]

The purpose of these lessons is to encourage more cognitive flexibility so that – via metacognition – we can stand back from our instinctive, fixed-mindset thoughts and challenge them. This way our students can maximise their ability to push the boundaries of their comfort zones and grow. The first stage is to become conscious of how thoughts impact on their everyday thinking and, therefore, on the feelings they have about themselves, their learning and their work. Metacognition helps students to manage their thinking more constructively, to take their automatic thinking less seriously and to see for themselves how to react to challenges with wisdom, empathy and grace.

Weaving the World Economic Forum skills into your curriculum

The skills in this book can, of course, be taught as discrete lessons to supplement personal, social, health and economic (PSHE) education and reinforce the crucial mindset for learning children will need at work and in life. I have taught all of these lessons as part of a Learning to Learn (L2L) programme for 13-year-olds and perceived a profound impact on their results and wellbeing. Even more effective is to identify how the skills are woven into the rest of the taught curriculum, and explore how they can feature and be highlighted in everyday lessons and in projects that bring learning alive for every child.

Curriculum design is a bit beyond the scope of this book, but if you are looking for ideas about how to overhaul your offering, I'd recommend reading *A Curriculum of Hope* by Debra Kidd and *The Monkey-Proof Box* by Jonathan Lear.[31] These books

---

30 Berners-Lee, *There Is No Planet B*, p. 185.

31 D. Kidd, *A Curriculum of Hope: As Rich in Humanity as in Knowledge* (Carmarthen: Independent Thinking Press, 2020); J. Lear, *The Monkey-Proof Box: Curriculum Design for Building Knowledge, Developing Creative Thinking and Promoting Independence* (Carmarthen: Independent Thinking Press, 2019).

contain excellent ideas for projects that are full of wonder and engagement. To conclude this introduction, I have borrowed some ideas from Debra and Jonathan to show how the skills in this book can be woven into cross-curricular projects to promote curiosity and commitment from students and teachers alike.

Jonathan Lear outlines the essential structure of curriculum planning as: skills progression – content and concepts – enquiry question – authentic outcomes and critical audience – critique.[32] I show in the examples that follow how the individual lessons in this book can fit into his beautifully simple model.

Project ideas

Having worked in primary and secondary schools, and having taught a variety of subjects, I remain passionate about providing an exciting, challenging curriculum for 9- to 14-year-olds. Children in this age group are at an exciting stage of developing their curiosity and autonomy, so we have an opportunity to help our students become addicted to challenge and learning. Better this than to simply allow this time to be used as preparation for SATs or GCSEs, as it can be in UK.

Offering themed learning across subjects such as English, the humanities, maths, geography, science, art and drama provides students with opportunities to connect and reinforce the skills that this book seeks to develop. In secondary schools, engaging several departments in planning projects that link up themes can serve to reinforce the learning and expand the students' schemas. The lessons in this book can support the learning process, whatever the project. A couple of examples follow.

My amazing brain

It has always been puzzling to me that we don't teach children how their brains work. The amazing brain project encourages children to explore what their brains are doing when learning. I have taught this many times to primary and secondary age children and they are always fascinated by the subject. It links closely to science and PSHE education but can also link to maths, English and history through the tasks.

---

32 Lear, *The Monkey-Proof Box*, p. 75.

My Amazing Brain	
What do we already know? Map out all they know about the brain and how they use it.	**Use:** Lesson 3
Focus on skill progression in: Metacognition, teamwork, research using technology and texts, thinking skills, managing memory, self-regulation, L2L.	
Content and concepts: Construction and workings of the brain. What we know about how learning works in the brain. Mental health and how it is affected by negative automatic thoughts (NATs). How learning works in humans. Parts of the brain. Neural pathways. Piaget, Pavlov, Dweck. How children learn language. Mental health and ill health. Texts such as *The Little Book of Big Stuff About the Brain*.[33]	**Use:** Lessons 1–6 Lessons 13 and 14 Lessons 33–36
Enquiry question: Does learning really grow our brain?	
Associated rich vocabulary: Intelligence, neuroscience, psychology, neurons, dendrites, synapses, subconscious, connections, memory, self-regulation, metacognition, plasticity.	

Activities:
 Students to:
     Create own research materials to use with peers.
     Write a student guide to maximising brainpower.
	Use:
	 Lesson 5
	 Lesson 11
	 Lesson 33

---

33 Curran, *The Little Book of Big Stuff About the Brain*.

Get feedback from peers on this guide. Create a short film, podcast or documentary programme for teens containing information and guidance about how to maximise their brainpower. Include dealing with anxiety and unhelpful thinking.	Lesson 36

Enrichment:

Arrange visits from a psychologist, neuroscientist or counsellor.

Students carry out a case study, teaching a younger child or interviewing an adult about their learning experiences.

Invite the visiting psychologist and an audience of peers to critique the film/podcast/documentary.

Authentic outcomes and critical audience:

Link their work to their local context, the real world and the problems that some of their peers may face. Present their performance outcome to an authentic audience of children, parents and experts.

Review and reflection:

Students create tests and quizzes to do either on their own or in groups after these lessons and activities to review the material and monitor their progress in developing metacognitive skills and gaining knowledge about learning and the brain.

Critique:

Raising expectations and standards. Students to review their own progress and record what they have learned and how they will use it in future. They can create a learning journal to use from now on.

Global warming

Global Warming – Save our Mother Earth	
What do we already know? Map out all they know about the problem and possible solutions.	**Use:** Lesson 2
Focus on skills progression in: Critical thinking, investigation, complex problem solving, data analysis, evaluation, experimental design.	

Content and concepts:
CO_2 emissions – sources and effects, such as:
  Air and sea heating.
  Ocean acidification.
  Glaciers melting.
  Sea level rise.
  Weather patterns changing.
  Deforestation/desertification.
  Permafrost melting and methane release.
  Extinctions of animals and plants/loss of biodiversity.
	Use:
	Lessons 6 and 8 (adapt subject material)

Associated rich vocabulary: See above. Also: rainforest, indigenous, evolution, sustainability, emissions, insolation, empathy.	

Activities:
Students to:
  Investigate recycling in their households and communities.
  Investigate renewable energy. Interview neighbours with solar panels to discuss advantages.
  Research and review materials and articles on global warming.
	Use:
	Lesson 9
	Lesson 11
	Lesson 16
	Lessons 24 and 26

Develop argued opinions for and against not taking a flight for a holiday.

Compose and write letters to political authority figures expressing concern about animals that are becoming extinct due to global warming.

Find out about the decline of the Amazon rainforest.

Enquiry question:

Would the world be better off without us?

Enrichment:

Organise a marketplace activity to discover most effective ways of cutting down emissions.[34] Visit a science museum. Read relevant poetry – for example, Donna Ashworth.[35]

Students to:

Write a relevant story – for example, about the Australian bush fires.

Plan a holiday for an ecotourist.

Hold a debate on the enquiry question.

Write a letter to the local newspaper suggesting six ways in which everyone can combat global warming.

Invite a local climate change activism group.

Invite local politicians to present policies to combat global warming.

Authentic outcomes and critical audience:

Students to:

Perform a dance/drama piece to persuade young children to be aware of their role in global warming.

Join/organise a protest or a litter pick in the locality.

Plant a tree.

---

34 See www.jackiebeere.com for materials for a marketplace activity on cutting CO_2 emissions.

35 https://ladiespassiton.com.

Review and reflection:

Students to:

Create tests and quizzes for themselves and their group after these lessons and activities to review material and monitor progress.

Quiz their family and community.

Review their progress and record what they have learned and how they will use it in future.

Create a personal action plan for the future. What would their ideal life look like on a planet where humans were in harmony with nature?

Critique:

Give kind, specific, helpful feedback on each other's performance.

Debra Kidd reminds us the importance of stories that anchor the themes of the curriculum content to the real lives of the children.[36] She also remarks on the simple wisdom of Ben Newmark: 'Our curriculum should whisper to our children that "… you belong. You did not come from nowhere. You are one of us. All this came before you, and one day you might add to it."'[37]

Outstanding schools feel so good because everyone – from the children to the teachers to the caretakers – feels a sense of belonging and pride in 'their' school. The curriculum must connect us to our community, our country and our heritage. If it does, then it will build the body of knowledge and the cultural capital that delivers a sense of who we really are and of our place in the world, and also inspire us to be the very best that we can be.

---

36 Kidd, *A Curriculum of Hope*, p. 27.

37 Kidd, *A Curriculum of Hope*, p. 23, quoting B. Newmark, Why Teach? *BENNEWMARK* [blog] (10 February 2019). Available at: https://bennewmark.wordpress.com/2019/02/10/why-teach.

Part 1

Active learning and learning strategies

Lesson 1

Your amazing brain

> **Aim:** To get curious about how your brain works and its amazing power.

Brain quiz – are these statements true or false?

1.   An adult brain has about 100 billion (100,000,000,000 or 100 thousand million) neurons (brain cells).

2.   Signals in your neurons can travel at the same speed as Formula 1 cars (roughly 100 metres per second or 360 kilometres per hour).

3.   Your neurons create and send more messages than all the phones in the entire world.

4.   You learn by making connections between neurons.

5. Exercise can help you learn.

6. An adult brain weighs about 1.3 kilograms (almost 3 pounds).

7. Your brain uses up 20% of your energy.

8. Learning makes your brain more powerful.

9. Your brain is more complex and powerful than any computer ever built.

10. Your brain still works when you are asleep.[1]

> A bee has 900 brain cells and a brain the size of a grain of salt.

TASK

What does a bee's brain do? Write a list of all the things a bee's brain has to think about in order for the bee to survive.

Now brainstorm all the things *your* brain has to do in a large learning map. (It might help to think about taking in information from the senses, processing it and then telling the body what to do.)

---

1 https://www.natgeokids.com/uk/discover/science/general-science/human-brain/; Queensland Brain Institute, 10 amazing facts about the brain (31 July 2018). Available at: https://qbi.uq.edu.au/10-amazing-facts-about-brain.

Lesson 2

Three brains in one

 Aim: To understand how brains work so that you can increase your ability to self-regulate.

The triune, or three-part, brain theory was developed by Dr Paul MacLean in the 1950s.[2] This is a long time ago, but it is still a useful model to help us understand our reactions and how learning works. MacLean suggested that there are three parts to the brain:

P – Primitive brain – also known as the reptilian brain, responsible for monitoring personal survival and 'fight or flight' instinct.

E – Emotional brain – governed by the limbic system, which is located in the centre of the brain, it's responsible for memory, emotion, values.

---

2   P. D. MacLean, *The Triune Brain in Evolution: Role in Paleocerebral Functions* (New York: Plenum, 1990). For more information, see: S-J. Blakemore, *Inventing Ourselves: The Secret Life of the Teenage Brain* (London: Transworld Publishers, 2019).

T – Thinking brain – the neocortex (thinking cap) where higher order thinking skills and those governing speech take place.

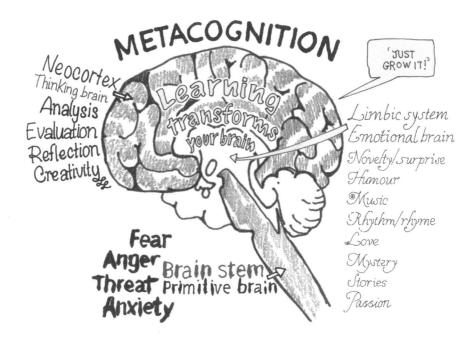

The P.E.T. acronym makes it easier to remember.

Make a 'brain' by holding both your fists together with your thumbs pointing towards your chest. Envisage the thumbs as the reptilian brain stem. Open them up and wiggle your fingers, to demonstrate the emotional brain. The knuckles on top represent the 'thinking cap' where all the hard work takes place. However, all three are inextricably linked and need each other for learning.

Your primitive brain keeps your body functioning and helps you survive. It is called the reptilian brain because this part is well-developed in all reptiles. If you are feeling threatened or stressed, it 'kicks in' and can take over. Reptilian brain state can make you get ready to fight, freeze or want to run away without you consciously thinking about it. (Think about what happens to your body if something unexpected frightens you.)

Look at this example to see another way in which the reptilian brain can work:

Andy was on lesson report, so he was working hard on his maths. The teacher left the room for a minute but just as she came back in, a ruler went flying past her head! Andy

looked up from his work and she wrongly accused him of throwing it. He went reptilian. He shouted back at her, slammed his fist on the desk and got sent to the head teacher.

TASK

Discuss or write down how Andy could have controlled his reptilian brain and what alternative reaction he could have had.

Now consider these questions. Think about your initial, instinctual reaction and then think about how you would react if you controlled that impulse. What would *you* do:

- if a teacher picked on you unfairly?
- if someone insulted one of your family members?
- if you were challenged by your parents about using your phone or playing a computer game too much?
- if you saw someone bullying another person?

Road rage is an example of when adults go into reptilian brain state. What do you think happens and why?

Think of three examples of situations in which you or someone you know went 'reptilian'. Can you think of any examples which involve social media?

Write down three ways to calm down and make a positive outcome more likely.

Think about what you could say to yourself to control anger. Try these slogans:

'It is what it is.'

'Oh well.'

'Next.'

'It's not worth it.'

'It's not about me.'

'Chill.'

'Relax.'

Or you could try counting to 10.

If these don't work for you, why not write another set of slogans to say to yourself to control anger?

Getting angry is a habit that is not worth the energy and it hardly ever solves problems. Keeping a cool head will always help you solve problems more quickly and effectively.

 What to do if you feel reptilian? *Use metacognition to stand back from feelings. (See Lesson 33.)*

Lesson 3

Your emotional brain

Aim: To understand more about your emotional brain and how to use it to become an effective learner.

The limbic system

This part of your brain runs your emotions. It stores memories, sets your values and beliefs, and is very important in learning. Your emotional brain loves praise, music, rhyme, colour, humour, novelty, enthusiasm and needs to see the point of learning and remembering stuff.

Just because the teacher taught it, it doesn't mean you will remember it!

Top tips:

- Make learning and remembering exciting, colourful, funny, and musical. Think of ways to do this with tests coming up … *now*.

- Give yourself a reason for learning and remembering. If you think it is important and care about it, it will count.

- Set yourself goals for learning and remembering stuff and reward your efforts.

- Use your imagination to help you become a better learner with a more powerful memory.

- Use your imagination to help you be more successful at sport or when performing.

Reflection:

Many famous sports stars 'train' in their heads, visualising a superb performance to make it happen. How can you use your emotional brain to help you learn?

TASK

It's much easier to remember emotional experiences than facts. Try it.

- Recall your earliest childhood memory and share it with a partner.

- Now recall any nursery rhymes or songs you can remember from your childhood.

Remember: Learning is emotional …

- Which are your favourite lessons and teachers? Why?

- Can you link the reasons you gave in your previous answer to your emotional brain?

Write your success story *now*. Describe a day in your life when everything goes brilliantly and you are a superstar – especially at learning. Start like this: 'I woke up and the sun was shining. I felt great about the day ahead because …'

It doesn't matter if your story seems unlikely or impossible. The more extreme you make it the better!

Now act out your day in groups of three or four.

Lesson 4

Your thinking brain

 Aim: To understand how brains work naturally to solve problems and to challenge yourself to develop cognitive flexibility.

The thinking brain (the neocortex) is your 'thinking cap' where all the hard work takes place.

There are different types of thinking, which we need to use in combination to make best use of our brains. Standing back and thinking about how we are thinking is called metacognition, and this is a useful strategy to draw on. (See Lesson 33.)

For example, when we are doing a jigsaw puzzle, we sort out the pieces using colour and shape, but we also use our brains to think about the 'big picture' and how it all fits together to get it right.

When you have a game to play or piece of furniture to build you can follow the instructions *or* just have a go at figuring it out. Which strategy do you use? Why?

TASK

To help understand the way your brain works, respond to these statements with Yes or No.

1. I organise facts and material well.

2. I work step by step.

3. I am rarely impatient.

4. I read instructions before starting.

5. I like to work things out on paper.

6. I like working on my own.

7. I like to make lists.

8. I can concentrate for a long time.

9. I like reading.

10. I enjoy working with numbers.

More Yes than No? You may be more of a logical thinker.

Now look at these statements. Do they apply to you? Respond Yes or No.

11. I prefer variety and excitement.

12. I like to doodle a lot.

13. I love trying new ideas.

14. I think of creative solutions.

15. I like new experiences.

16. I just try out ideas as I go along.

17. I prefer to flick through a magazine starting at the back.

18. I make decisions based on gut feelings.

19. I find it hard to concentrate for long periods of time.

20. I prefer art to reading and maths.

More Yes than No? You may be more of a creative thinker.

If you have a fairly equal number of Yes and No answers to all 20 questions, you are in the middle – which is an excellent place to be because you are using logical and creative thinking. This will make you a great learner.

Two kinds of thinking

Logical	Creative
writing	ideas
logic	intuition
numbers	daydreams
analysing	sport
reading	playing music
sequencing	the big picture
language	rhythm
detail	colour
spelling	imagination

TASK

We can get into habits that can help or hinder our ability to learn. It's important to challenge your thinking habits so that you are a flexible thinker. Think about how you can get into the habit of using both sides of your brain while learning.

- How could you use more creative thinking in maths?
- How could you use more logical thinking in drama or art?

Look at the following list of tips to help get you into good habits for learning.

Top tips for logical thinkers:

- You may need to be more open to trying new activities and ideas.
- Don't get bogged down in detail.
- Practise working well with others.
- Vary your learning habits to keep your creative brain working.
- Know that making mistakes is an important part of learning.

Top tips for creative thinkers:

- Remember the details – take one step at a time.
- Create lists to ensure you get things done.
- Make yourself do some planning and prioritising in advance.
- Avoid procrastination (putting things off!).
- Avoid distraction and distracting others.
- Don't rush in without thinking.
- Read the instructions and check your work when finished.

Find out more about the brain processes involved in learning and memory and how they work.

Lesson 5

Brain boosters

Aim: Use physical activities to give your brain a break and boost your performance.

Remember: Your brain needs food, oxygen, water and sleep. Sleep helps the brain process everything that happens during the day and it is vital that you get enough of this.

Also, during the day, it's good to have a physical break sometimes when learning, so try these exercises:

- Stand up, stretch, reach up and breathe deeply to give your brain oxygen.
- Rub your tummy with one hand, pat your head with the other.
- Do the twist – arms one way, legs the other way.
- Lift your knee and touch it with the opposite hand. Repeat on the other side. Alternate quickly.

- Draw a large figure of eight in the air with one finger. Draw another large figure of eight with the other finger going the other way – make sure your fingers don't touch!

- Trace out the number 10 in the air, with one hand creating the 1 and the other hand the 0. Try it with 27, 39 and your age.

- Turn your head slowly from side to side, roll your shoulders gently and lift your arms up to grow as tall as you can.

- Roll down and touch your toes. Hang your folded arms and swing them gently to stretch your spine. Roll back up one vertebra at a time.

- Stand on one leg with your knee bent in a right angle, while stretching your arms out on each side for balance. Stay as long as you can then change legs. Try this with your eyes closed – it's hard!

In the air or on paper:

- Write your full name with your wrong hand in large letters.

- Write your name with both hands, creating a mirror image.

- Try writing your name backwards with your wrong hand.

- Write the name of your favourite band, country and food – using your wrong hand.

- Create an impressive signature then copy it with your wrong hand.

- Throw your pen from one hand to the other and back again.

Boost your brain by trying something new every day. A food you don't eat, a TV programme you never watch, a person you don't usually speak to – make new connections!

Dancing is a brain booster. Choreograph a simple dance with friends and practise it for 30 minutes to boost your working memory.

Michael Mosley[3]

---

3   M. Mosley, The Truth About … Getting Fit, *BBC One* (22 January 2020).

TASK

Have a brain/body workout

Imagine that you are at the gym and a huge set of weights is in front of you. *In your mind*, see yourself in full gym kit looking strong and happy, bending your knees and picking up the weights. See yourself lift the weights and straighten your legs, keeping your back straight. Then raise the weights to your shoulders. Feel the weight, feel your strength. When you are steady, lift them above your head and straighten your arms. Feel the weight for a few seconds then carefully lower them back to your shoulders. Raise them ten times, then place them carefully back on the floor. This mental exercise can make you stronger in the real world.[4]

Review

Write down five things you have learned from this lesson.

Write down three action points which will help you to develop your learning strategies.

---

4   I. Robertson, *Mind Sculpture: Your Brain's Untapped Potential* (London: Bantam Press, 1999).

Part 2
Complex problem solving

Lesson 6

Connect with your inner baby

 Aim: To practise problem solving.

 # TASK

What serious problems and challenges does a newborn baby face?

List all the skills a baby learns before the age of 3.

Take one of those skills and write a paragraph, illustrated with diagrams, that gives a step-by-step description of how a baby learns it. Show what personal qualities will help children to develop these skills.

Now consider a person from the Stone Age (or choose a different period that you've studied). Describe a challenge they would face and a problem that they would have to solve. For example, creating a tool that could increase their hunting and gathering efficiency.

Create a flow chart that shows how to tackle the problem. For example:

| PROBLEM. We need tools to make it easier to kill animals for food. | Make a sharp weapon that can kill quickly and easily. | I could use a big sharp flint stone but I don't want to be close to the animal I'm killing. | Attach the flint to a long wooden stick using leather straps. I've invented the spear! |

Now choose one of these real, modern-day problems to solve:

- Too many cars in the country.
- Too much carbon dioxide in the air, causing global warming.
- Too little money to run your school.

You can work in pairs or groups.

Top tips:

- Define the problem. What are its causes and effects? Try to list as many as you can.

- Be a creative thinker to solve the problem. Try the 100 solutions strategy in Lesson 7.

- You can also use the 5 Whys model to explore the problem in depth. For example:

Lesson 7

100 solutions

 Aim: To take a problem and work as a group to consider lots of possible solutions.

Analytical thinkers need to be cool, calm and objective, with great attention to detail. Asking the right questions is an important skill.

Creative thinkers take risks *and* challenge their minds to think outside of the box.

TASK

Start with a real-world problem that is affecting your school or local area. For example: 'A shortage of teachers' or 'Litter is ruining our parks'.

First, be a creative thinker:

Simply brainstorm 100 ideas in a group and write them down on a big piece of paper. Don't worry about whether your ideas are realistic or practical; they can be as wild and wacky as you like.

Choose your five favourite solutions to the problem, remembering to involve everyone in the discussion and decision.

Then be an analytical thinker:

Imagine that you are a detective or scientist working on the problem. Look at the five solutions you just came up with. Switch off your emotional brain. Be focused, practical and unbiased as you examine each solution and test each one out using a SWOT test. For each solution look at its:

Strengths

Weaknesses

Opportunities

Threats

Based on this analysis, throw out all but two of the solutions, then do some market research for each one. Take the remaining two solutions to other people in the class and ask them for their opinions. Use this to choose what they think is the best one.

Now create a proposal or advertisement to sell your solution to people. Make sure this explains clearly why it is the best option.

Present this solution to the class.

Lesson 8
Plus, Minus, Interesting

 Aim: Practise a strategy that will allow you to think through any subject and see beyond any prejudices and preconceptions.

Complex problem solving involves seeing all sides of a situation.

For example, on the topic of 'London', you might make the following observations:

INTERESTING
The population is highly
educated: 60% of
working-age people
have a degree.
There is an ethnically
diverse population.

PLUS
It has historical significance.
There are many tourist
atttractions to visit.
It is an international
financial centre.

MINUS
It is noisy and
overpopulated.
Food, drink and housing are
very expensive.
There are many queues.

TASK

See what you already know about any subject using this thinking tool.

Gather some newspapers and apply this Plus, Minus, Interesting approach to the news.

What conclusions can you gather from this exercise about the content of newspapers?

Part 3
Critical thinking

Lesson 9

Asking the right questions

Aim: To understand how important questioning is and how to form good questions.

Build your brainpower

You learn more from asking questions than from answering them. To ask questions you need to be creative in your thinking. You need to work from back to front.

A good question pushes back the boundaries of knowledge and shows you are engaging your brain with learning.

TASK

If this is the answer ...?

If these are the answers, think of three possible questions for each statement.

For example: Yes, we have no bananas. 'Are there any fruits you find hard to get in your shop at the moment?'

- There must be another way.
- I haven't stopped dancing yet.
- My computer does it for me.

Now, in pairs, think of three more answers and get your partner to think of the questions.

Share the best examples with the class.

Work with your partner to create two or three questions on each of the following topics using the 8Way Thinking Tool (see page 57).

- Global warming.
- Social media.
- Skateboarding.
- The moon.

Can you answer any of your questions? Can anyone else? How can you tell whether they are useful questions?

Write down the definition of a useful question for learning.

Using the 8Way Thinking Tool

Write an idea under each heading that relates to your topic. Use internet research to help you. Here is one example for each 'thinking way' related to the topic of global warming to get you started:

- Feelings: Sadness

- Actions: Recycling
- Sounds: Crackle of forest fires
- Numbers: 2-degree rise in temperature
- Sights: Tsunamis
- Nature: Glaciers melting
- People: David Attenborough
- Words: Extinction

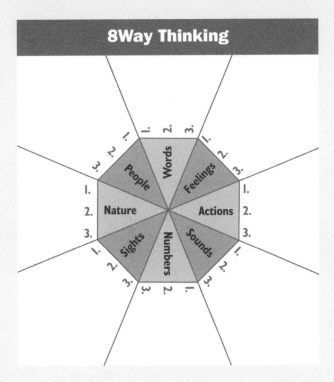

Under interrogation

Being good at asking questions is important in many professions. Imagine that you are a suspect in a case of burglary in your home area. Your partner is to interrogate you. Create ten crucial questions to ask about the event that will move the case forward. Try them out then swap roles.

Lesson 10

Dealing with confrontation

 Aim: To understand how losing your temper is just your brain reacting to your thinking and creating feelings – and to invent some strategies for self-regulation.

- Critical thinking helps you stop and think clearly about how to respond to a situation.

- Critical thinkers employ good reasoning to get to the truth and choose what to do.

- Being able to change your behaviour by having better understanding is one way critical thinking can help you with challenges.

- Confrontation is a perfect situation in which to apply critical thinking.

Our brains are built to protect us from danger, and if you are feeling threatened or stressed then panic can kick in and can take over. Your primitive survival brain state can make you take flight (run away), fight or freeze. This state of mind is a throwback to our evolutionary programming, so we sometimes call it 'going reptilian'. Whatever you call it, it can stop you thinking logically and sensibly about a situation. Critical thinking skills help you to stand back, keep calm and work out what to do for the best.

Consider this example:

Taz likes school because he sees his friends and has a laugh. Now he is in Year 8 he gets away with being a bit cheeky to the teachers. When he was younger, he worried about getting good reports but now his friends' approval seems so much more important. He has a gang to hang around with and they always kick a ball around at break. Last week it was hot, so they all took their shirts off. Taz is a bit shorter and a lot thinner than his mates and they started calling him 'Tarzan' to be funny. It wasn't nice and after a while he lost it and kicked his mate where it hurts, so they all ran off and left him alone. Since then they've kept sending him pictures of skinny boys from Instagram and laughing emojis. Now Taz doesn't want to go to school and he has sworn at his sister and smashed her best doll. His mum is furious and doesn't know why he's shut himself in his room.

TASK

Pause to think before you react

Discuss or write down an alternative reaction for Taz.

Metacognition (see Lesson 33) involves standing back from your emotional response and thinking carefully, critically and rationally about your thoughts. How could this help Taz?

Can social media make you less confident or even angry? How and why? Discuss your opinions or write an answer explaining your view.

Consider other problems students might face, and how critical thinking could help them to handle the situation more effectively. Write a letter detailing a specific problem. Get into groups or pairs and swap problems. Write back with a sensible answer, offering advice.

Losing your temper can lead you into trouble

Consider this scenario:

You are in a queue waiting to buy some sweets at the cinema. It's taking ages and the film starts soon. You don't want to miss it so you're feeling tense. Just as you reach the front of the queue someone walks straight in front of you and pushes in. You elbow them out of the way and demand to be served first. The cashier is upset by your attitude so serves the other person. You throw the pack of sweets at them and swear. Before you can make it into the film screening you are escorted out of the building by security, who threaten to call the police because you are shouting and struggling.

Talk through or write down your version of events.

Imagine you are the cashier and write down an account of what happened from your point of view. Alternatively, you could create a voice recording.

Lesson 11

Peer critique

 Aim: To practise how to critique a friend's work so that they can improve it.

Being able to critique each other's work in an objective way that uses assessment criteria will help you learn to give specific, helpful advice about how to improve. (Assessment criteria are the things you look for that make a piece of work good.) Do this when work has been assessed by the teacher or feedback has been given to the class. Watch the YouTube video of Austin's butterfly, which demonstrates beautifully how well even very young children can critique each other's work. Be kind, helpful and specific when giving feedback.[1]

---

1   R. Berger, Critique and Feedback: The Story of Austin's Butterfly [video] (8 December 2012). Available at: www.youtube.com/watch?v=hqh1MRWZjms.

TASK

Self-portrait

On a blank piece of A4 paper draw a large head and shoulders self-portrait in 90 seconds with whichever hand you don't normally write with. To be successful this picture must look as much like you as possible and fill the page.

When complete, swap the portrait with your neighbour, who should write, on the back of it, one piece of praise and three pieces of advice to improve the drawing so that it meets the success criteria (i.e. looks like you).

Swap them back and act on the feedback you are given. Then hand your portrait to the teacher. The teacher can randomly distribute the portraits among the class to see who can recognise the artist and return each portrait to its correct owner.

Did you get your portrait back? How many in the class got theirs back? How helpful was the feedback? Were you surprised by how successful you were in doing what seemed like an impossible task?

How did it affect your attitude to the task to be told you must draw:

- a self-portrait?
- in 90 seconds?
- with your wrong hand?

Explain how your emotions changed during this task. How did you feel at each stage?

Now try drawing a self-portrait with the hand you normally write with. Compare the pictures. What was the difference in how you felt about each activity? Can you think of another challenging task like this to try?

Rate my advice

Draw your pet, or the pet you would love to have. Redraft it three times after seeking advice from your peer critique partner. How does getting feedback from your peer help you to improve? Give your peer critique partner a mark out of ten based on how helpful their advice was. What could they do to improve their advice?

Part 4
Creativity

Lesson 12

Out of the box

Aim: To grow your confidence so you feel able to take risks.

TASK

First, complete the following table.

	Would do	Might do	Would never do
Complete a parachute jump			
Travel by train alone			

	Would do	Might do	Would never do
Pick up a spider			
Complain about a product in a shop or café			
Backpack to Australia			
Go to a party alone			
Speak up against a group when I disagree			
Film myself singing and put the video on YouTube			

Now take your 'would never do' list and write statements to describe your thinking – like the examples in these speech bubbles:

Now write a bucket list of 20 things every child should do by the time they are 15. Make them varied, exciting and challenging – things that will push them outside their comfort zones. Here are some examples:

Change the world – starting with me			
Make someone smile (and every day!).	Stare at the stars.	Grow something to eat.	Cook a meal for someone else.
Learn a poem by heart.	Watch a film made before you were born.	Climb a tree.	Learn some song lyrics from the 1960s.
Watch and discuss the news.	Learn to count in another language.	Sort out a bag of your stuff and take it to a charity shop.	Walk a journey instead of going by car.
Try a new food.	Tell someone what they mean to you.	Bake a cake.	Do a household chore.
Choreograph and perform a dance.	Read a book or magazine you have never read before.	Work out your monthly expenditure.	Study a famous painting.

Lesson 13
Confidence boot camp

> ➜ **Aim:** To find out about ways of building self-confidence.

START

You feel more confident about trying something new.

Do something new that challenges you.

Your brain learns to adapt and grow.

Make mistakes, get it wrong and then put it right.

TASK

Boot camp

Create a weekend boot-camp programme to help children of your age to build up their courage and open their minds. You will need to employ lots of creative thinking to design tasks that will make your campers fearless. The camp should have all sorts of challenges: physical, emotional and intellectual. List them under those headings.

Now design some publicity material to convince your peers to come on the course and explain how they would benefit.

Feel the fear

Think of five scary things that you would find difficult to do. Discuss what would make you do them. Would you pick up a big spider? Would you do it to save someone's life?

Explain why you should challenge yourself to do things that are hard and different.

The importance of failure

'There is no such thing as failure, only feedback.' What would it mean if you applied this belief in your life? How can you make failure into success?

J. K. Rowling wrote the hugely successful Harry Potter books, but she had many failures on the way to her success. Here's part of a speech she made to Harvard University graduates:

Failure gave me an inner security that I had never attained by passing examinations. Failure taught me things about myself that I could have learned no other way. I discovered that I had a strong will, and more discipline than I had suspected.[1]

---

1 J. K. Rowling, 'The Fringe Benefits of Failure, and the Importance of Imagination', transcript from *The Harvard Gazette* (5 June 2008). Available at: https://news.harvard.edu/gazette/story/2008/06/text-of-j-k-rowling-speech/.

Research some other famous successful people who also experienced failure in their journey to success.

Write and perform a one-minute speech entitled: 'Failure is even more important than success.'

Lesson 14

Out of your comfort zone

Aim: To inspire you to push yourself out of your comfort zone.

Reflection:

What is the bravest thing you have ever done?

What have you done that has taken some courage?

What would you do if the wing of the plane you were in caught fire?

What would you do if someone called for help from behind a wall?

None of us know how brave we would be in an emergency, but in the long run it really is important to be brave in your own life and constantly push yourself out of your comfort zone. This means being open to new ideas and activities.

TASK

Comfort, challenge and panic zones

Draw three concentric circles and list examples of things you normally do inside the centre one. This is your comfort zone. List things you find uncomfortable in the second circle. Label this 'My challenge zone'. Put things that *really* scare you in the third circle. Label this 'My panic zone'.

'Life begins at the edge of your comfort zone.'

Design a poster for your bedroom that illustrates this mantra.

Reflection:

What are you scared of?

What presses your panic buttons?

What happens to your body?

What is a phobia? Name some phobias.

Why do people get phobias? How can they overcome them?

Fear of failure prevents lots of us from pushing the limits of our comfort zone and achieving more. But if we can get comfortable with feeling afraid and still go ahead and challenge ourselves, our comfort zone gets bigger. Why? We are afraid of less and we have grown more confidence to tackle new challenges.

The moment that we see that every feeling is just the shadow of a thought, we stop being scared of our feelings and just feel them.

Michael Neill[2]

---

2 M. Neill, *The Inside-Out Revolution: The Only Thing You Need to Know to Change Your Life Forever* (London: Hay House, 2013), p. 108.

FEAR = Fantasised Experiences Appearing Real

TASK

How to have courage

Choose something from outside of your comfort zone circle that you would like to do.

Now take control of your thinking and self-talk. Give yourself motivation by thinking of reasons why you want to do it. Imagine yourself doing it – and loving it. Visualise how you will feel when you have done it.

Here's the challenging bit (this will take courage!). Stand up and explain to the class what courageous thing you would like to do and why. Describe doing it in the present tense for a couple of sentences.

The more you push yourself out of your comfort zone, the stronger and braver you will become.

Make FEAR = Feel Everything And Recover.

Know that emotions come and go. Let them wash over you. Don't overreact to feelings. We all feel afraid sometimes. It's human and it's OK to feel it.

Create some thought bubbles that will give you courage when you need it most.

Personal challenge

Create a board game based around snakes and ladders. You can only move up your ladders if you complete the creative challenges you set yourself, such as sing a song or finish that piece of artwork. You can think of unhelpful thoughts and write them down in speech bubbles – for example, 'I can't draw' or 'I'm bored'. These are your snakes that take you down the board and slow your progress.

Thunks

Thunks are questions that challenge your perceptions and get you to think in a different way. They were created by Ian Gilbert, and a vast collection can be found in *The Little Book of Thunks*[3] and *The Compleat Thunks Book*.[4]

Here are some thought-provoking Thunks to try:

If you always got what you wished for would you always be happy?

What has the most freedom – an ant or a schoolchild?

Is a person who has a face transplant still the same person?

Which is heavier, an inflated or deflated balloon?

Is love invisible?

Can being sad make you happy?

Can you experience fear without being scared?

Here are some more thought-provoking questions:

What colour is Tuesday?

What does sadness taste like?

Discuss your answers with a partner or in a group.

Can you think of three more?

3 I. Gilbert, *The Little Book of Thunks: 260 Questions to Make Your Brain Go Ouch!* (Carmarthen: Crown House Publishing, 2007).
4 I. Gilbert, *The Compleat Thunks Book* (Carmarthen: Independent Thinking Press, 2017).

Tap into your senses

 Aim: To understand that your thoughts can create feelings – and that this is OK.

- Imagine a puppy sitting on the desk in front of you.
- Write down exactly what it looks like and what it is doing. See yourself playing with it and picking it up.
- Now change the puppy into a snake. Does this feel different?

TASK

Cinema screen imagination

In pairs, take it in turns to shut your eyes and describe the walls of your classroom to each other.

Then recall your last lesson. Describe what you can see in your mind in as much detail as you can.

Give your partner a mark out of ten for the amount they can remember.

Now recall the best lesson/experience you have ever had. Make the picture in your head bright and colourful and as big as a cinema screen. Describe it to each other in pairs. How does it make you feel to see it in your head?

Draw a spider diagram/doodle of that lesson with images and words that capture the atmosphere.

Do you remember it better in words or pictures?

Put some lively, familiar music on. Ask the teacher if you can use your headphones for this or if they can play some music for the whole class. Write down or draw all the visual images that come into your head.

The moving eye test

Look straight at your partner's eyes. Draw an arrow to show which direction their eyes move when you pose these questions/challenges:

What colour is your front door?

Imagine seeing a purple lion.

How many people and animals live at your house?

What would I look like with blue hair?

What would an elephant squeaking sound like?

Think of your favourite song and listen to it in your head.

Some people think that your eyes move to a different place when you look inside your head for information, or lie, or try to imagine something. What do you think? Make up four more questions to test out eye movement. See where your eyes go when you are telling the truth and looking in your memory bank and notice if they go in a different direction when you are imagining things. It depends on whether you are right- or left-handed but there might be a consistent direction for recalling information, lying or using our imaginations. Get curious about this!

Create your own virtual reality

Give your visual imagination a workout every day by daydreaming a situation in which you are the hero of a success story or when something you are worried about goes well, such as an exam or a meeting.

Try doing this now. Put some soft music on and set the scene in your head. (This works even better if you try a relaxation exercise first – for example, the mindfulness activity in Lesson 34.)

Now draw a picture or write an account of this story to remind yourself. Then repeat your visualisation.

You can use this to help deepen your learning too. Run through your lessons and remember what you have learned.

 Moreover, repetition has other benefits for our brain: it automates our mental operations until they become unconscious.

Stanislas Dehaene[5]

Turn movies on in your head when you read

If you can make pictures in your mind it can help you understand what you read, and this will help you in exams. Visualising the content can help you to comprehend it.

5   Dehaene, *How We Learn*, p. 220.

Read this passage from *Unforgettable Places to See Before You Die* by Steve Davey.[6]

---

1. As you stand in the cold darkness of an Arizona night, waiting for dawn, you will have no comprehension of the enormity of the landscape in front of you. In the dull early light your first view of the Grand Canyon will be a flat, almost painterly composition.

2. Then gradually the sky turns to blue and red, and golden sunlight starts to pick out details – first the edge of the far ridge, then the tallest pinnacles inside the canyon itself.

3. As the sun rises higher, more is revealed. Rock formations sculpted by years of erosion are illuminated, and long, convoluted shadows are cast on to giant screens formed by cliffs.

4. Only when you notice details, such as a row of trees, or a flock of geese flying overhead, do you come to realize the true scale of the canyon. That far ridge might be 15 km away, and the mighty Colorado River – a mere stream viewed from above – is 1500 metres below.

For each numbered paragraph:

• Create a picture in your head.

• Draw a picture on paper to show what is in your mind.

• Add extra details that make it more interesting but still fit with the text.

• Describe what is in each picture to your neighbour.

Test how this technique can improve your memory and understanding by describing what is happening in the following passages from Act 5, Scene 5 of *Macbeth*.

---

1. 'Tomorrow, and tomorrow, and tomorrow,
    Creeps in this petty pace from day to day,
    To the last syllable of recorded time;

2. And all our yesterdays have lighted fools the

---

6   S. Davey, *Unforgettable Places to See Before You Die* (London: BBC Books, 2004), pp. 36–37.

way to dusty death. Out, out, brief candle!

Life's but a walking shadow; a poor player,

That struts and frets his hour upon the stage,

And then is heard no more:

3. *It is a tale*

   Told by an idiot, full of sound and fury,

   Signifying nothing.[7]

Make each section into an image or a film in your mind.

Describe to your neighbour what is in each visual and why.

See how much of the quote and its meaning you can remember.

Create an abstract scribble drawing that represents what this quote means to you. How does imagination affect your mood?

The more you practise visualising and talking about those pictures the easier you will find it to remember things and understand meanings.

---

7 W. Shakespeare, *Macbeth* (Project Gutenberg edition, 1998 [1623]). Available at: https://www.gutenberg.org/files/1533/1533-h/1533-h.htm.

Part 5

Leadership and social influence

Lesson 16

Empathy – put yourself in someone else's shoes

 Aim: To practise showing empathy and complimenting others.

Empathy is the ability to see another person's point of view and understand their feelings.

Great communicators get on well with others – including people they don't know. This is often because they have empathy with the people they communicate with. Sometimes they show this consciously but often it is an unconscious thing. In the same way, successful people try to understand others in order to work well in teams and become good leaders.

How good are you at working with others? Could you have more empathy?

How well do you get on with:

- your friends? (easy)
- your sisters and brothers? (harder)
- your mum and dad/carers? (can be hard)
- your teachers? (very hard)
- your neighbours? (harder still)
- people you don't know yet? (hardest)

TASK

Empathy glasses

Make a pair of empathy glasses from card. Put them on when you need to make a conscious decision to see another person's viewpoint. (Or, in real life, pretend to put them on when talking to people.)

In pairs, choose one of the following statements. You each have one minute to give your honest opinion on the topic:

- Students should be paid to go to school.
- Parents should be allowed to smack their children.
- Drugs should be legalised.
- Bullies should be forgiven.
- There should be no homework for children.

Then put on your empathy glasses and argue the opposite view. Score each other's empathy factor out of ten.

Role-plays are a good way of improving communication and empathy.

Neighbourhood nightmare

In a group, take on the roles of an old pensioner, a young vandal, the village police officer, the school caretaker and so on. Each gives a statement about the trouble that has been going on in the village. Then swap roles and look at it from a different point of view.

Learn to compliment others

Write down individual compliments about five other members of your class (not just your friends!) and one about your teacher.

Take it in turns to volunteer to deliver the compliments and mean them. It is just as important to accept compliments from others by making eye contact, smiling and saying thank you.

In a group, think of six ways of helping someone else to succeed or be happy. Present your ideas to the class.

Can you be charming?

 Aim: To practise building rapport.

Rapport is a French term which means getting on together. If you can establish rapport it makes people more likely to like you from the first meeting. It means you know how to be charming and can communicate in effective ways. Body language matters when establishing rapport.

You can improve your ability to build rapport by:

- Working with as many different people every day as you can – don't just work with your friends.

- Actively making new friends. Don't wait for people to talk to you.

TASK

Win them over

Practise rapport and charm with a partner who you don't know. Ask them three questions about themselves.

Top tips:

- Keep your body language open, maintain eye contact, and smile and nod.
- Keep your shoulders back and head up.
- Mirror their position.
- Listen carefully to what they say and feed back to show you understand.
- Ask questions with interest and listen closely to the answers.
- Check you've heard them by paraphrasing what they say.
- Remember to show empathy when you can.

Ask them to score you out of 10 based on how good your listening and rapport building was. Do they have any advice for you to improve? Now swap roles and repeat.

Sell your pencil

One of the greatest tests of your ability to generate rapport is to try to sell something.

Work with a partner, using your best rapport-building skills to convince them that they need to buy your pencil from you. You have one minute.

Get feedback about how you did and how you could improve. Try again – this time, sell something else on your desk.

EXTENSION TASK

Challenge your rapport-building skills. Research a charity and find out how you could raise funds by creating a mini campaign as a group. This could be a garage sale, a sponsored event or some community fundraisers such as car washes or gardening jobs. See who can raise the most funds for their chosen charity.

Lesson 18

Understanding others

 Aim: To explore what forgiveness means to you.

Sometimes people behave badly and upset you. It will happen at school, at home and at work. How you respond to such situations is the key to happiness. Grudges grind you down, so being able to forgive and move forward without blaming yourself or feeling angry is a powerful strategy.

TASK

Forgiving is very hard. Bearing grudges is very easy. In a group, discuss if this is true. Why?

Now discuss which of these statements you agree with and why:

- Everyone deserves forgiveness.
- Forgiving can help you move on.
- Forgiving is weak.
- To forgive is to be strong.
- Forgive and forget.
- Forgiving is more important for little things.
- Grudges grind you down.
- If you forgive it means it could happen again.
- Forgiving makes you feel good.
- Forgiving yourself is most important.

Share your group's thoughts with the class. What happens when you can't forgive someone and you bear a grudge? How do you feel? List your emotions.

Make up six more questions about forgiveness, such as: How does it feel to forgive? Why should I forgive?

Then think of a real-life event that made you feel angry. Write down the story of what happened or tell it to your neighbour. Now answer each of your six questions and relate it to your story.

What do think of this statement? 'If people behave badly, it is because they are scared or insecure.' Discuss.

Being fair means being able to weigh up what is right and wrong and, consequently, make a good decision.

You can't change what has happened, but you can change how you feel about it.

Grudge is small and mean and angry.

Forgiveness is big and generous and kind.

Forgiveness and fairness go together.

With the above portrayals of Grudge and Forgiveness in mind, draw an animal or a humanoid creature to represent Forgiveness and one to represent Grudge.

A Community of Enquiry is a group discussion or debate with certain rules – such as taking turns, respecting each other's views and helping everyone contribute. It is better if the class sits in a circle and manages this without the teacher leading the discussion. So, as a class (or a large group) hold a Community of Enquiry discussion in a circle about 'fairness' in these situations:

- A footballer takes a dive and gets someone else a red card.
- A teacher gives the whole class a detention because a few children are too noisy.
- A dog has to be put down because it bites a child.
- A dolphin chokes on a plastic bag.
- The food that you throw away in your bin could feed starving families. Can those families forgive you for throwing perfectly good food away?

EXTENSION TASK

Look up 'fair trade' on the internet and find out more about what it means. Find out what fair trade products your local shops stock.

Respect yourself and others

 Aim: To learn about how your actions impact on how you feel, and make others feel.

The first person you have to respect is yourself. What you say to yourself in your own thinking has a massive influence on how you see yourself. Ask yourself this question: Am I a success?

Think about this for a minute.

Did you have an argument with yourself? Maybe your thinking went something like this: 'Yes, I'm a success and I've done well in X, Y and Z most of the time, but I've often been useless at A, B and C. I am kind and thoughtful about others – mostly …' And so on …

Try to focus on the best bits about you. Think also about how you can improve the things that need to be improved. Believe you can become more successful. This is one way to get self-respect.

Also realise that, every day, something you do or say will make someone else feel good or bad. Make sure you spread happiness when you are working with others by:

- Being a good listener.
- Having empathy.
- Speaking up and helping others to have their say.
- Making others feel that you care about their feelings.

People will forget what you say, people will forget what you do but people will never forget how you made them feel.

Attributed to Maya Angelou

Know your NATs

NATs are negative automatic thoughts that can swoop into your mind. Imagine someone says or does something you don't like. The NATs swoop in very quickly (in 3 milliseconds) and before you know it you end up reacting by going 'reptilian' and saying or doing something that you later regret. This can happen even between friends.

Become aware of your NATs and try to practise pressing the 'pause' button to give you time to let them go, so that you can react differently.

Remember, how you react to stuff determines how other people see you.

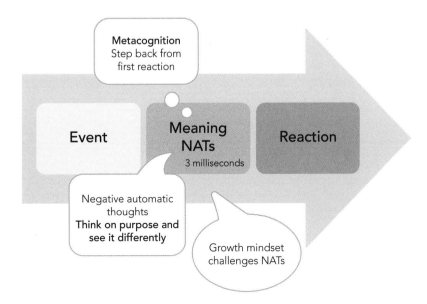

The more you can handle your NATs and respect yourself and others, the better a team player and leader you can be. It will also make you stronger and more confident.

TASK

Respect

Think of three people you respect.

- What makes you respect them?
- What actions make you respect yourself?
- What actions make you respect someone else?

How can you earn respect from your friends?

What does respect look like? How is it different from having manners or being polite? In the following table, list the behaviours and attitudes that relate to good manners, self-respect, respect from others, and being polite.

Good manners	Self-respect	Respect from others	Being polite

Create a shield that shows your personal values using pictures and words. Show your shield to the class and describe what it means.

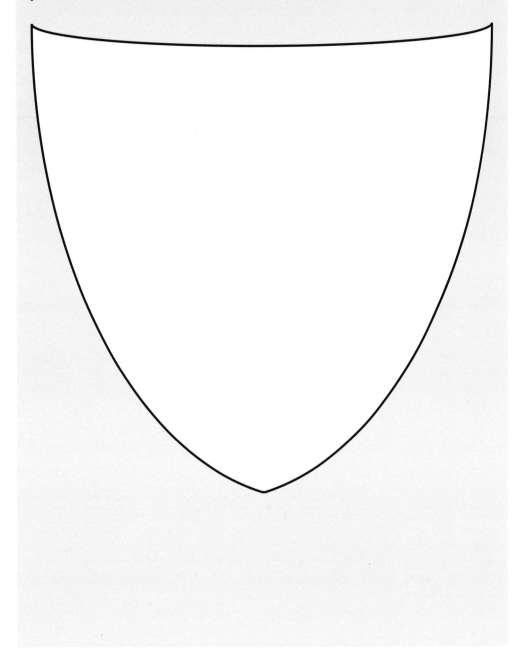

Peer pressure

Make up some more thought bubbles or speech bubbles to represent the dilemmas of self-respect versus group respect.

Part 6

Emotional intelligence

Test your EQ

 Aim: To review your EQ (emotional intelligence) and set yourself targets.

Have you got what it takes to be a winner? EQ is more important than brainpower in determining whether you will be a success in school and in life.

TASK

Test yourself

In response to the following ten questions, score each quality out of five according to how often you feel it applies to you. 5 means 'Always', 1 means 'Never'. Be honest!

1.   Do you take responsibility and set goals for the future?

2.   Have you got confidence and self-belief?

3.   Are you persistent?

4.   Are you an optimist who sees the positive side of things?

5.   Do you take care of your health and fitness?

6.   Do you have willpower and self-discipline?

7.   Have you got the courage to try new things?

8.   Do you work well with others and listen carefully to them?

9.   Are you good at planning and organising your work?

10. Do you keep calm when difficult things happen?

Swap your answers with a friend and see if they agree with your self-scoring. Discuss your answers.

You can improve your EQ – and become a winner.

Choose your three lowest scores, then create a target sheet to plan how you will improve your EQ.

Understanding your strengths and weaknesses will help you succeed.

Target your EQ

For example, let's say you're not so good at 1, 7 and 9. You could make a table like this:

EQ target	Action needed to develop better habits	Slogans and sayings that will help motivate me
1. I must take responsibility for my own life and set goals for the future.	No excuses. Accept responsibility. Review where I am and plan where I want to be. Don't blame anyone else. Get organised – make a plan and monitor it every week. Don't be afraid to make mistakes, because you can learn from them.	If it's to be, it's up to me. If I can dream it, I can do it. I can't control what happens, but I can control how I think about it.
7. I must be braver and take more risks.	Give myself little challenges and do things that scare me. Walk a different way to school. Volunteer for a club. Do a presentation that I wouldn't normally do. Say yes to a request for help.	Do something that scares me every day. What doesn't kill me makes me stronger. Every mistake is a learning experience.

EQ target	Action needed to develop better habits	Slogans and sayings that will help motivate me
9. I must organise myself better and prioritise and plan.	Make lists every day of what I need to do and tick them off as I do them. Check my bag is packed with all the right stuff. Use my phone to remind me of deadlines and important events. Avoid displacement activity, such as messaging mates or surfing the net to put off doing unpleasant jobs.	Do the worst first. Work smarter, not harder.

Now it's your turn to create your own target table.

Lesson 21

Get to know your best friend: you!

 Aim: To get to know yourself, and how your mind works.

You can control your thinking and your inner voice to get what you want in life, and it starts with understanding how your mind works. Many of your thoughts and feelings come from your unconscious mind. The following diagram is based on the Freudian theory of mind.

Conscious
mind

Preconscious mind –
recent experiences

Beliefs, values, instincts, fears

When you think, you
rehearse everything you do
using pictures and words.

Your conscious inner voice
can really help motivate you
– or make you worry.

The way in which your
unconscious mind is
programmed affects all you do.

Thoughts often start
from what is within your
unconscious mind.

Make sure you have some
good beliefs and values that
can feed into your decisions.

Don't let unfounded fears stop
you trying to reach your goals.

Feelings come from thoughts

Your emotions are normal. We all have days when we feel sad or happy.

Don't take your thoughts too seriously, because they sometimes hold you back.

This lesson will help develop your *intrapersonal* intelligence, so you can be more self-reflective. Just thinking about the questions that follow will help you understand your unconscious mind and how your thinking makes you feel.

It takes courage to be honest about yourself, so decide now whether you are brave enough!

TASK

Question time

Look at the following questions and consider your answers carefully.

1. What do you do when you are angry?
2. What makes you feel sad?
3. When was the last time you laughed out loud and when was the last time you cried?
4. What three things would you like to do (but haven't yet) and why?
5. Who would you talk to if you had a major worry?
6. How well do you cope when someone criticises you?
7. How do you cheer yourself up when you are in a bad mood?
8. When was the last time you couldn't get your way about something important and what did you do?
9. What do you do when you get stuck on a question at school?
10. How would you describe your personality?

Discuss your answers with a partner and see what similarities and differences there might be between your responses.

Choose a few answers. Write them down on a piece of paper and fold it up. Pass your answers to another pair and ask them to write down the questions that they relate to. Then discuss it as a foursome and see how many you got right.

What three things have you learned about yourself from this task?

If you didn't learn anything that says something about you too!

Be kind to yourself

This is the most important thing you will do today!

Think of a positive thing to say to yourself every day when you look in the mirror. Write it down on a sticky note and put it somewhere to remind you. Say it in your head. Louder!

Give it a kind, lovely voice. Say it again.

Say it every day. Mean it!

When in doubt, ask that kind, helpful voice what to do.

Beliefs and values

Use the following prompts and questions to investigate your beliefs and values:

Write down three things which you believe are important for happiness – your own and everyone else's.

If you won £1 million what would you spend it on?

What qualities do you value in a friend?

Now ask three other people of different ages for their answers and compare them with your own. Report the results of your survey to the rest of your class.

Every week write down three things that make you glad to be *you*.

Optimism – get the golden glow

 Aim: To learn to reframe (not flip) your view of a situation.

Consider this story …

Once there was a rich father with two daughters: one was a pessimist and the other an optimist. One Christmas he asked them both to draw up a list of all the presents they could wish for. He bought the pessimist everything on her list, wrapped the presents up and put them in her bedroom on Christmas Eve. He bought the optimist a lorry load of manure and put it at the foot of her bed on the night before Christmas.

On Christmas morning he was astonished to hear his pessimistic child crying and his optimistic child whooping in delight.

'What's wrong?' he asked the pessimist. 'You got all these lovely presents ...'

'Yes, but now I have all these lovely presents, all my friends are going to be jealous and hate me. And ... and ...' sobbed the pessimist, 'how am I ever going to have the time to play with all these lovely things?'

Sighing, the father went to his other child – who was laughing and jumping about in glee.

'What did you get for Christmas that has made you so happy?' he asked.

'I got a load of manure ... and it's all at the end of my bed ... whoopeee!' she shrieked.

'Why does that make you so happy?'

'Well, I figure that with this much manure around there must be a pony waiting for me somewhere ...'

Reflection:

This story can make you think about these questions:

Can you change the way you think?

Is optimism a habit?

Can you turn any situation around by thinking about it differently? This is called reframing – it is a very useful thinking tool.

Find reasons why these typically negative events *could* be seen as a good thing:

- Breaking your arm.
- Moving house.
- Getting a low mark on a test.
- Losing your phone.
- Falling out with a friend.

Where are you on the mood monitor?

Low   1   2   3   4   5   6   7   8   9   10   High

Optimism is infectious. Try to spread happiness – not misery!

Optimism is all about seeing the positive side of a situation. Try to find the silver lining in every cloud. Make this a habit.

Have you got the habit of optimism? If you have, you will be more successful in life – and live longer.

What you say with your inner voice and what you say to others creates your way of thinking. Look at the table that follows. What are you more likely to think or say?

Negative	Positive
This is really boring.	This is interesting.
I can't do this.	I enjoyed that lesson.
No one likes me.	My mates are great.
It's raining again.	It's a lovely day.
That's typical.	That's unfortunate.
Just my luck.	I'm just born lucky.
I hate maths.	Learning stuff is great.
Teachers hate me.	Teachers like me.
Everyone picks on me.	I'm brilliant.
I'm not eating that!	I'll eat anything!
School is a waste of time.	I'm really trying to do this.

Remember: We all get in a bad mood sometimes. What matters is accepting that moods come and go; they are just the result of our thoughts. If we don't dwell on negative thinking, we can take the steps to change our mood for the better.

 The day doesn't create your mood, your mood creates your day.

Practice makes positive

It might seem cool to be negative about everything – especially school – but if you are pessimistic and negative, you will programme or train your brain to switch off. If you say something often enough you will believe it! If you are optimistic and positive, you will become a great learner.

Look again at the table on page 109. Think of some more sayings for each column.

Try saying the positive statements in lots of different ways – you will find yourself feeling good just by saying them.

Now take each negative statement and think of a positive response to turn it around. For example, you could add 'but …'

Optimism cake

Create a recipe for optimism cake. Include the important ingredients that make people feel positive and the quantities needed. Draw a picture of the cake to show what it might look like.

Ingredients	Amounts

Top tips to get the golden glow of optimism

- Smile! Research shows that people who smile a lot are more successful in life. Try it *now*.

- Compliment others. Do it every day. Make people feel better after they have met you.

- Use social media in a positive, supportive way to make others feel good. How could you do this?

- Whenever you have a negative thought, *reframe* it and see the silver lining. There is always one there! Try saying:

  » It could be much worse.

  » I can learn something from this.

  » It will make me stronger as I learn strategies to cope with this and my brain makes new connections.

  » What doesn't kill me makes me stronger!

TASK

Sparkling story

Write a story about a time when you sparkled – a time when you were at your very best. Exaggerate it and write it in the present tense. For example: 'It's a wonderful spring day, I wake up, yawn and glance in the mirror. I look fresh, smiley and ready for a brilliant day …'

List all the good things in your life. Pin this on your bedroom wall. Look at your list when you feel down.

Create a gratitude diary. Every day, write down three things that went well, made you happy or that you are grateful for. For example:

- Today it was sunny.

- I played for the netball team and scored a goal.

- My mum got a new job, so we had a celebration dinner together.

Smile

Say something optimistic to your friend before you leave the lesson. Leave the classroom smiling and smile at three people you don't know at break.

Get together with friends and deliberately fake a laughing fit. You may find it makes you laugh for real. When you laugh, your brain chemistry changes and puts you in a better mood.

Lesson 23
Get a growth mindset

 Aim: To understand how and when to use a growth mindset for learning.

The way you think and how you respond to events can be called your mindset. A famous psychologist called Carol Dweck researched the mindsets of thousands of children and adults to discover what made them successful (or not) in school, work and life.[1] She found that people who knew when to use a growth mindset focused on learning when struggling with a challenge.

When we have a fixed mindset we tend to think that people are born with a fixed amount of intelligence and a defined personality and that not much can be done to change them. People with a growth mindset tend to believe that their intelligence can grow and that their personality can also change over time.

We are all a mix of growth and fixed mindset – the secret is to know when to apply your growth mindset thinking.

---

1 Dweck, *Mindset.*

TASK

Test yourself

Do you agree or disagree with the following statements? Score yourself on a scale of 1 to 10: 1 if you completely agree, 10 if you completely disagree. Then add up your scores.

1.   You have a certain amount of intelligence, and you really can't do much to change it.

2.   You are a certain kind of person, and there is not much that can be done to change that.

3.   You can learn new things, but you can't really change your basic intelligence.

4.   You can do things differently, but the important parts of who you are can't really be changed.

The more you disagree with these statements – i.e. the closer your score is to 40 – the more growth mindset you are. Being growth mindset works best for learning in the long run.

But you can always change your mindset. Ask yourself *which* mindset helps you when you are stuck.

Check out what makes *you* feel clever

Fixed mindset – I feel clever when:	Growth mindset – I feel clever when:
I don't make any mistakes.	I try really hard and learn to do something I couldn't do before.
I finish something fast and it's perfect.	I work on something for a long time and start to figure it out.

Fixed mindset – I feel clever when:	Growth mindset – I feel clever when:
Something is easy for me, but other people can't do it.	I listen to feedback on things I got wrong and learn how to put them right.
I come top of the class in a test.	I work with someone new and learn from them.

If you have a fixed mindset, you might feel a need to get things right straightaway, so that others can see that you are clever and talented. It makes you feel good to be able to get things right, but mistakes and failures make you feel very worried. This fear of failure makes you want to stay in your comfort zone and makes you unwilling to challenge yourself in case you don't look clever. With a fixed mindset, you can also be very certain about your views of people and events. You don't want to consider changing your mind.

If you have a growth mindset, it's fine to make mistakes and get it wrong at first. Fear of failure is not a problem, so you can take on challenges outside of your comfort zone and enjoy them. You don't mind if it takes time to learn new things and make progress, as long as you're finding useful strategies to help you. You love getting feedback from friends and teachers and then using it to improve. People with a growth mindset thrive when they're stretching themselves. They see struggle as growth. They are willing to consider changing their opinions or views after listening to others.

Having a growth mindset means you are willing to learn and grow. You know mistakes are OK because you can learn from them.

Remember: We are all sometimes growth and sometimes fixed mindset.

 All the lessons in this book will help you develop a growth mindset.

TASK

Fixed and growth mindset thinking

We are all a mixture of both – it's good to recognise what your thinking habits are.

You have a maths test today.

Draw two faces: one to represent a fixed mindset, the other to represent a growth mindset. Draw a big thought bubble next to each of them. In each one, write down a fixed and a growth mindset response to the following events:

The teacher asks you to speak in assembly.

You get dropped from the netball team.

Your friend gets angry with you for eating meat as he has become a vegan.

You usually come top in the spelling test but today you came 15th.

Your teacher has marked your story and said it's not up to your usual standard.

Today it's time to learn Spanish for the first time.

Take your learning home

Make a poster for your bedroom wall that has lots of growth mindset sayings. For example:

> Every mistake is a learning experience.
>
> My brain can grow.
>
> Failing is an important part of learning.
>
> The harder I work, the cleverer I will get.

Part 7

Judgement and decision making

Values for success in life

 Aim: To use your own values to guide you to make good choices.

Values are the things we care about the most. Some people value money and possessions; some people value their family and friends the most. For some people, their religion or beliefs are the most important thing in their lives.

 Reflection:

What do you value?

Who do you value most in the world?

What does your country value?

What values do you appreciate in a friend?

What values does a good team leader have?

TASK

Values for life?

To what extent do you agree with the following statements? Give yourself a score out of 5: 1 being completely disagree, 5 being completely agree.

1. I know what my values are.

2. My values help me decide what to do when I have problems.

3. I have opinions on most things.

4. I know what I want in life.

5. I know what my school values.

6. If someone asks me to do something that I don't feel is right, I say no.

Telling your story

In pairs, take it in turns to tell a story from childhood that shows how and why you changed your mind about something important.

Now think about how you might react if faced with a challenging situation. What would you do if:

- you found an injured cat in the road?
- you found your friend crying?
- your friend suggested that you bunk off school for the day?
- you saw an older child threatening a younger child?
- you found a purse on the floor in a shop?

Compare your reactions with your partner and discuss any differences in your responses. What do you think this reveals about your values?

Family and friends matter

 Aim: To review and understand what you value in your personal relationships.

 Reflection:

How has your family influenced you?

How do your friends influence you?

Are there any areas of conflict between friends and family?

What are the differences between real friends and online friends?

TASK

Qualities and conflicts

Which of the following qualities do you most appreciate in friends and family? Can you think of any others?

loyalty	discipline	good looks	cleverness	coolness
sense of humour	generosity	good listener	musicality	popularity
time for you	strength	rich	optimism	love

Draw a table like the one below and list the qualities under the relevant heading. You can list the same quality twice if it is important in both friends and family.

Friends	Family

Write an advert for a best friend that you could place on social media – a friend who would support you to be happy and successful.

What qualities would they have?

Wanted: best friend. Must ...

Social media can have a good or a bad impact on friendships and on the ways in which we communicate with each other. Write some advice to a young relative who you care about, assuming that they have just got their first smartphone. Is there anything you wish you had known when you first got a phone?

How can you be a better friend or family member? Write down five things you can do today.

How do you handle it when you fall out with someone? What are some of the causes of conflict?

Things friends fall out about	Things families fall out about

Choose one of the triggers for arguments from your lists. Role-play the conflict in a group and show two versions – a positive outcome and a negative outcome.

Golden rules

Now think about what helps people to get on with each other.

Create five golden rules for family harmony.

Create five golden rules for friendship.

Problem solved?

Write a problem page for a children's or teenage magazine with three different problems about friendship – and then write the answers. Read each other's problem pages and see if you agree with the advice.

Lesson 26

I can choose

 Aim: To understand your own power of choice.

This value is about your own personal power of choice – the power you have when you choose to forgive others, to be happy, to think positively, to show empathy, to communicate well …

But with power comes responsibility. Your greatest responsibility is to yourself.

How good are you at doing what *you* want?

Rate yourself (honestly) based on how much you would be influenced by what others in your peer group think of the following. Score yourself out of 5: 1 for not influenced at all, 5 for very highly influenced.

1. The clothes you buy.

2. The music you listen to.

3. The friends you have.

4. Your hobbies and interests.

5. The lessons you like.

6. How hard you work at school.

7. The teachers you get on with.

8. Your attitude to your parents.

9. Your career ambitions.

10. How you spend your free time.

Write some sentences that sum up the main influences in your life when you see how you have answered these.

Then see if this fits with the answers you give to the following reflection questions.

Reflection:

Who is in control of your life?

How can peer groups influence you in negative ways?

How can you be strong and stick to your values?

Who, actually, chooses how much influence others have on you?

TASK

Peer pressure versus values

How many of your friends today will still be your friends in a year's time? How about in ten years' time?

Describe the qualities of the friends who will still be around.

Create a group role-play that shows a gang planning to commit a crime. Show how members of the gang influence each other to do things that they would never do alone.

Why do some people say cruel things on social media that they wouldn't say in real life?

Knife crimes and acid attacks are sometimes carried out by young people. Would they commit these offences without the influence of 'friends'?

What are the differences between gangs and friendship groups?

How and why does power corrupt? Think of how this relates to history, politics, family, friends.

If it's to be, it's up to me

Personal power means taking responsibility. It means making no excuses and no blaming others.

Forgive yourself when you get it wrong and just learn from it.

Know that you can make great choices. They are *your* choices.

You are as perfectly wise, resilient and resourceful as you let yourself be. It's *your* choice!

 # TASK

You versus excuses

Write down five excuses for not doing your homework.

Write down five excuses for not tidying your room.

Write down five things you want in life.

Write down five excuses for not getting them.

Now write down five things you want and the reasons why you are determined to get them.

Are these things important in life? They were your choice – do you choose to change your list if you decide that they are not?

 You have the power to make these excuses or not. 'I can choose' – say that to yourself every day.

Let go of things you *can't* control

Sometimes it's important to realise that there will be some situations that are outside of your control. Recognising what you can and can't control is really important. Start by drawing two concentric circles. In the inner circle, list the things you can control; list the things you can't control in the outer circle. Here is an example to look at after you have tried thinking about your own life.

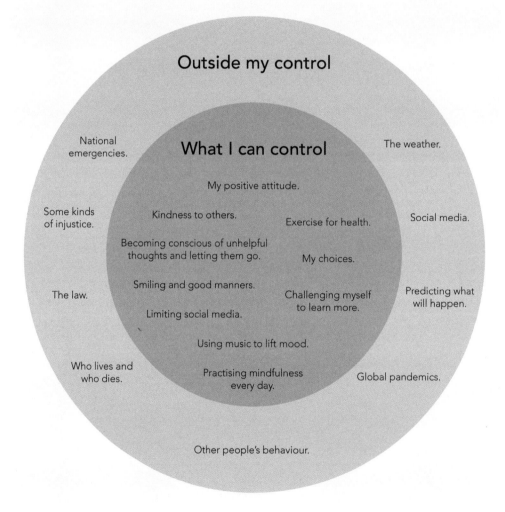

Outside my control

National emergencies.

The weather.

What I can control

My positive attitude.

Kindness to others.

Exercise for health.

Some kinds of injustice.

Social media.

Becoming conscious of unhelpful thoughts and letting them go.

My choices.

Smiling and good manners.

The law.

Challenging myself to learn more.

Predicting what will happen.

Limiting social media.

Using music to lift mood.

Who lives and who dies.

Practising mindfulness every day.

Global pandemics.

Other people's behaviour.

Part 8
Service orientation

Lesson 27

The 3Es: Enterprise, Energy, Effort

 Aim: To learn to use the formula Enterprise + Energy + Effort = success.

Enterprise means you are not scared to take a risk. You have the courage and willingness to do a difficult task – and can think of new and original solutions. You take the initiative. You do not wait for someone else to go first.

Energy means you are lively and enthusiastic and can work hard for a long time in order to get what you want.

Effort is about the hard work and resilience it takes to make a difference and overcome difficulties. You can have dreams to be a footballer or a musician, but research shows that the only way to really achieve a high level of skill is to put in lots of practice – some estimates suggest as much as 10,000 hours.[1]

Reflection:

What is the opposite of the 3Es?

Why will having both enterprise *and* energy, *and* putting in the effort, make you unstoppable?

TASK

What does success look like?

Research two or three people who been successful in business and write up their stories. Look for the 3Es.

Create a mini business that will raise money for your favourite charity. It could be anything from selling cakes to a car washing business or inventing an app. What will it take to succeed?

Dragons' Den

This is based on the popular BBC TV show. Vote for the three to five most enterprising and energetic people in the class to be the Dragons. They each have up to £50,000 (of imaginary money) to invest in each group. The Dragons will work out their backstories (education and careers), decide on the types of business that they are keen to invest in and prepare criteria for how they will judge the groups that are asking for investment.

The groups of two or three will need to invent a product to sell to the Dragons, or promote the charity business that they have created. Each group will prepare

---

1 M. Gladwell, *Outliers: The Story of Success* (London: Allen Lane, 2008).

a three-minute presentation with the intention of convincing the Dragons to invest in them. The winning group will be the one that attracts the most investment.

The Dragons also have to give positive feedback on how each group delivered on the 3Es.

Self-assessment and peer critique

How did you all do on the 3Es – enterprise, energy and effort?

Write up a short kind, specific and helpful review of each team member's performance and share them with each other.

Lesson 28
Social intelligence

 Aim: To become aware of how body language, voice and tonality can create or break rapport.

Social intelligence helps you to feel confident with people, make friends and be a great communicator. How you communicate is one of the most important skills to develop for work and for life. But communication isn't just about what you say (though that's important), it's also about *how* you say it – your tone of voice, facial expression, eye contact and general body language.

TASK

It's how you said it ...

In pairs, say the following sentences with different tones of voice and different body language and facial expressions. Really mix them up to change (or confuse) the meaning:

Hopefully, this shows the importance to the listener of how you say things, not just what you say.

Discuss the sort of situations in which you might think or say these things. What messages are you giving? What do we mean by a bad attitude?

Turn it around

Now write an account of a time you had bad service from someone with a bad attitude. Make one up if you need to. Say how the experience made you feel.

Rewrite the experience with a change in the way you were served that would make you feel really good.

Draw out the speech bubbles but with the *opposite* view inside them.

Colour them in using bright colours and draw an appropriate cartoon face or character to show the attitude that they convey.

Attitude at work

Employers always stress the importance of a good attitude for success and career progression. How does someone with a 'good attitude' behave?

Take a look at this reference written about an employee who works at a retail store:

Kevin has an attitude problem that affects everything he does and says. He slouches around the workplace with a permanent sneer on his face. He is always looking at his phone, paying little attention to the job he is supposed to be doing. He has an unpleasant growl when spoken to by customers and shrugs his shoulders and walks away whenever a customer asks for help. He speaks to colleagues only when spoken to, avoiding any eye contact and replying in monosyllables and grunts. Kevin refuses to act on advice about how to do the job more effectively and often doesn't seem to be listening, even when being given important instructions about health and safety. No one wants to work with him.

I had no alternative but to ask him to leave the business.

Write the reference out again, this time saying the opposite things about Kevin: describing the behaviours of someone with a very positive attitude.

Lesson 29
An attitude of gratitude

 Aim: To reflect on how important gratitude is as part of your attitude in life.

 # TASK

How do you present yourself?

Rate yourself (out of five) based on how you think you present yourself. Be honest. 1 is completely disagree, 5 is completely agree.

I smile a lot.

I greet people in the morning even if I don't know them well.

I listen to others' views.

I like to do a job well.

I don't mind working hard.

I like to impress people.

I open doors for people or help them out.

People who come into contact with me go away feeling happier.

I am friendly to people I don't know.

I try to use my initiative if I am stuck.

I think it's important to keep learning.

I am open to new ideas.

I am grateful for the feedback people give me that helps me know how to improve.

Faking it to make it

Thinking about the personal qualities that you scored highly on, write yourself a letter of application for your dream job. Really exaggerate your positive attitude. Work the statements from the self-assessment task into your letter.

Include some quotations from people who have noticed your great attitude in the past. For example, 'Jaz always helps me in the garden, working hard to keep the paths clear of leaves and weeding the flower beds. She is cheerful and pleasant to visitors.'

Showing your gratitude

Write down three things that you are grateful for about the place where you live and the people who live close by.

Now think about what you can offer others. Who could you serve in your community? Neighbours, family, local businesses, care homes, etc.? What could you do that would make a difference and help?

Plan a service project to deliver in your local area.

Write a letter that proposes the project. Create an action plan to present to the class.

Pausing for perspective

What should human beings be grateful for?

In 2020 a pandemic swept through the world. How can a pandemic that stops us going to school, taking holidays or socialising be something that can also make us grateful?

Part 9
Negotiation

Lesson 30

Be a good listener

 Aim: To understand the importance and power of listening.

Listening is a very important skill to acquire as so much of what you learn in school is presented by teachers talking to the class or explored through group discussions. When you become a good listener, you have more understanding of how other people see the world and this will also help you to be a good negotiator. Good listening requires attention and concentration, and it is respectful to listen carefully. Listening skills are vital to learning and to life. How can you be a better listener?

TASK

Listening

Listen to the sounds around you now – jot down everything you can hear.

Now listen to your insides – what can you hear?

What makes a good listener?

Not really listening

Team up with a partner. Your partner has five counters or buttons in their hand and two minutes to tell you a story about something they really care about – maybe their favourite football team, television programme, etc.

You need to listen, but you also have to constantly interrupt their story by asking them questions designed to get them to say 'yes' or 'no'.

Each time the storyteller says yes or no, they have to give you a counter. The challenge is to see if you can get all five counters by getting the storyteller to say yes or no five times during their two-minute story.

Swap around the roles to see how many counters your partner can win off you.

Discuss how it felt to tell your story and get interrupted by someone who was trying to get you to say something else. This is an example of unhelpful listening.

Now try this:

Your partner tells the story of their favourite holiday for one minute. You really listen properly. Then repeat back as much as you can remember.

Swap around and do this again.

What differences did you and your partner notice about the way in which you were being listened to and how did it feel?

Listening practice

In pairs or individually, find out how good you are at listening. Here are some activities to try:

- Listen to a poem read out by the teacher – once. See how many words and phrases you can remember and jot down afterwards.
- Read out a shopping list with ten items and see how many your partner can remember.
- Play a piece of music or a pop song and really listen to it. Try singing the lyrics or humming the tune afterwards.

Listening to each other

Still in pairs, imagine that you are at a counselling session. One of you is the counsellor, one the client. Tell the counsellor your real (or imaginary) problems about school or home in three or four minutes. The counsellor then has to repeat back to you a summary of the problems and suggest some solutions.

We listen in our heads too!

Listen to your internal dialogue – the voice that talks to you inside your head whenever you think about stuff. It often gives you a running commentary on what you are doing and what you are going to do.

What sort of voice is it? Is it your voice?

Change the way it sounds. Is it normally miserable and complaining? If so, make it positive and encouraging. This can be very motivating. Try this by asking yourself how good you are at school. Listen to the voice. What is your self-talk saying? Make it positive. Make it say that the area in which you are struggling is an opportunity to grow!

How does this change make you feel? What did your inner voice just say? Was it positive?

Now imagine that you are asked to do a bungee jump for charity. How would you react?

Internal voice: 'I might die! People get injured. I might chicken out at the last minute and look like a fool.'

Positive voice: 'That could be exciting. I'm sure I can do it, and think how good it would make me feel! And I'll be raising money for a good cause.'

Which one is closer to how *you* think?

Make the most of self-talk to build confidence and self-belief.

Lesson 31
Communication skills matter

Aim: To understand the importance of how we communicate with others as part of a team.

The ability to work well as part of a team is one of the main skills that employers are seeking. Sometimes that means putting your own needs or views into the background for the good of others. It also means bringing out the best in others. You need to be able to work with all sorts of people – not just your friends. Think of two examples of times when you have enjoyed working or playing sport in a team. What made it work well?

TASK

Describe a time when you have been in a team. How did you contribute? What other team members impressed you? What makes a good team member? Write down three attributes of good team members.

Helping others succeed is a sure-fire way of raising your self-esteem. Every good deed you do will come back to you again and again, though not always straightaway. Be generous – you won't regret it in the long run.

TASK

Learn to give honest positive feedback to others – and mean it.

Write down six positive statements about members of your class, your teachers and your school.

Now sit face to face with a partner. Look them in the eye and say something nice about them. Take it in turns and notice how it feels to give and take compliments.

In a group, think of three ways in which you could improve the lives of the people in your home or school community.

Present your ideas to the class. Use visual aids if necessary.

Lesson 32

Body language

 Aim: To understand the impact of your communication on others.

Getting on with people – often called interpersonal intelligence – is one of the most important skills in life. However, much of what we do when we communicate is outside of our conscious awareness, so we may not realise what impression we are making on others.

TASK

How do you communicate?

It is often said that these percentages show what is important to the person you are communicating with:

Vocal: 38%

How you sound: volume, pitch, pace, intonation and energy.

Visual: 55%

How you look: posture, gestures, facial expressions, eye contact and clothing.

Content: 7%

What you say.[1]

Show these percentages as a diagram, pie chart or cartoon.

Does this change how you think about the way you say something?

Reflection:

When you first meet someone, what do you notice about them?

How long does it take you to form an opinion about whether or not you like someone new?

What impression do *you* make on people you meet for the first time? There are some people who are immediately likeable, so how would you make sure that you are one as well?

---

1   J. Thompson, Is Nonverbal Communication a Numbers Game?, *Psychology Today* (30 September 2011). Available at: https://www.psychologytoday.com/intl/blog/beyond-words/201109/is-nonverbal-communication-numbers-game.

Body language matters more than what you say. Body language is made up of:

- Your facial expressions.
- How you stand or sit.
- How much eye contact you make.
- Posture and gesture.
- How you shake hands.

Your body language is very important in making you feel confident.

TASK

Look confident

Think of someone who is confident. Describe their body language. Draw some stick men to show confident and anxious body posture. Draw some facial expressions too.

Volunteer to walk into the room with anxious and confident body language and see how it makes you feel. What do other people recognise in your body language?

The way you walk and talk can make you feel differently. When you feel worried you can change the way you feel by walking like your hero.

Positive body language also helps you to establish rapport with people you meet.

Talk in pairs about a holiday you would love to go on. Try to mirror each other's movements in a natural way and see how it feels.

Just a minute

In groups, take it in turns to speak for one minute about one of the following topics:

- Spiders.
- Chocolate.
- Traffic jams.
- Smartphones.
- Scooters.

Speak up and speak clearly, with strong body language, good eye contact and a smile. Give each other feedback with a focus on the body language rather than the content. Choose one person from your group to deliver their speech to the whole class.

 Top tip: From now on, think about how you impact on others. Practise getting and breaking rapport and ask for feedback from people about how you come across to them.

Look at the table that follows and circle the actions that you think would help you to build rapport.

Smile	Tilt your head sideways	Fold your arms	Turn your back	Slouch
Keep eye contact	Shoulders back	Frown	Raise your eyes to the sky	Speak clearly and with varied intonation
Look down	Have your hair flop in your eyes	Head up	Laugh	Tut

Play friendship speed dating

Sit opposite someone in your class (someone you don't really know, not a friend) and spend five minutes chatting and getting to know them better. Swap partners until you have spoken to five different people.

Afterwards, make notes (without mentioning names) about what it was that makes you want to grow a friendship with someone who you don't know very well.

Part 10

Cognitive flexibility

Lesson 33
Metacognition

 Aim: To understand more about how thinking works and how to stand back from your thinking to take control of your feelings.

There are many different definitions of the term 'metacognition' – it's often described as 'thinking about thinking'. It can be helpful to consider it as the act of standing back from thinking. It's a form of self-awareness that help us to reflect and become conscious of how our thinking works to create our experiences, our behaviour and, indeed, the way we learn.

This is important because it helps us to understand how our thoughts can create our feelings. We can take more control of our feelings by changing our thoughts.

Learn to stand back, reflect and reframe

Recognise your thoughts as bubbles that constantly float into your mind. You can either focus on them and grow them or let them go. It is useful to learn to dismiss or reframe worrying thoughts or limiting beliefs. What you focus on, you will strengthen. Always consider whether your thoughts are helpful or unhelpful. Don't waste energy on unhelpful thinking unless there is something to be learned from it. Anxiety can magnify unhelpful thoughts, but they are only thoughts.

Do you see good, evil or cool? Can you see all three? At the same time?

How do you change from seeing one word to seeing something else? Do you focus on different parts, squint a bit, close one eye?

You are playing with your *perception*. Everything that happens to you – everything that you see and experience – is framed by your perception: how you see it. Standing back and becoming aware of thoughts, this is the secret to *metacognition*.

TASK

What does it mean?
Beauty

Truth

Love

Success

Evil

Effort

Take each of these words and in a group of four or five discuss what each of them means to you, exactly. See if there are any differences of opinion within the group.

Discuss the following events and see if your group can agree on an order from most to least favourable:

1.   You don't get picked for the school team.
2.   Your friend comes top in a test.
3.   Your pet dies.
4.   You get a nasty message on social media.
5.   Your favourite toy breaks.
6.   You're offered a holiday abroad with a friend.
7.   You find a £20 note.
8.   Your best friend moves away.
9.   You win a spelling competition.
10. Your parents fall out.

Did you all have the same view, or did you need to argue your point?

Can you take one of the points that seems to be a bad thing and try to see it in a different way? Can you imagine how it could be a good thing?

Have you noticed that everyone sees things differently?

Social media

Discuss your experience of social media – Facebook, Instagram, etc.

How do you use it? How does it make you feel? What are the pros and cons?

Did you know that it actually makes people depressed to look at pictures on social media and compare themselves with others? It encourages us to judge ourselves and other people. Getting 'likes' gives us a quick dopamine hit (a hormone that gives us an instant 'feel-good' sensation), but these kinds of online interactions can feed our insecurities and don't always give us the longer lasting benefits that talking to people in real life does. In fact:

Heavy Facebook users show signs of being more gregarious, but they are also more likely to be anxious, hostile, or depressed.[1]

 How you see any situation will dictate how you feel about it.

Mind the NATs

If metacognition means that you can stand back and see any situation in a different way, you need to become aware of your thoughts and decide whether they are helpful or unhelpful. You can choose to think on purpose, and in a positive way, instead of letting your unhelpful negative automatic thoughts (NATs) rule. NATs come into your mind very quickly – almost without you noticing. The secret is to become conscious of them by pausing between the event and your reaction.

Example:

You enter your maths lesson late as you are dreading it. (NATs: 'It's going to be long and boring. I hate maths anyway. I don't like the teacher.') The teacher gives you the first task. (NATs: 'I can't do maths. I'm going to struggle with this.') You don't try and the teacher gets upset with you. (NAT: 'She hates me.') So, you answer the teacher back angrily without thinking. This situation leads to classroom conflict.

---

1   D. Rock, Your Brain on Facebook, *Harvard Business Review* (18 May 2012). Available at: https://hbr.org/2012/05/your-brain-on-facebook.

Alternative:

You enter your maths lesson early and greet the teacher. ('I might as well be cheerful as it might improve the day.') The first task is challenging. ('This is well hard; it must be growing my brain.') You ask the teacher for help and she shows you a new method and smiles at you. ('I think she likes it when I try.')

One NAT leads to another. But also, one good thought leads to another. It's how you respond that matters. You can probably think of at least one situation in which you could have changed your thinking and changed the outcome of an event.

If you use metacognition you can always stand back and think again. This creates a growth mindset and makes you emotionally intelligent: characteristics that will set you up to be happy and successful in life.

TASK

Write a story about an event when NATs nearly created a disastrous reaction. Include a commentary detailing what the NATs are saying to you.

Lesson 34
Mood control

 Aim: To understand how moods can be habits.

We all get in bad moods sometimes and these are usually created by our thoughts in the moment. *It will pass*. For example, you might be feeling really down and upset. Then something could happen that instantly changes your mood. You could get a phone call or text from a friend that makes you laugh, or you go for a walk in the sunshine and come across an excited puppy, or you get a hug from someone you love.

Choose to be in a good mood – you can be in a good mood if you want to be. Changing your thoughts, body language, activity, company and/or way of speaking can change your mood. In a good mood you will have more energy and courage.

There are many different types of mood: happiness, sadness, disgust, surprise, anger, fear, frustration, anxiety, hopelessness, fury, guilt, disappointment, loneliness, jealousy, calmness, curiosity, love, excitement, desire … to mention just a few!

Reflection:

What mood are you in? Can you help it?

What puts you in a good or a bad mood?

TASK

What's the mood?

Draw an arrow on this continuum to show where you think you are:

Despairing   Depressed   A bit down   OK   Quite good   Good   Great   Ecstatic

Explain to your neighbour why you placed yourself there and what contributed to you feeling like that.

The mood you are in can change the outcome of events. If you can understand and be OK with your moods, then you can control your life. Sadness, happiness and everything in between are part of life.

We all feel sad, happy, angry, bored, scared sometimes. These emotions are normal human feelings and often pass quite quickly. It's always good to talk about your feelings and realise they are OK. We can learn how to get ourselves into a happier state of mind more often, but if you feel low for a long time, talk to someone you trust and ask for help.

In pairs, take it in turns to put your hands in front of your face. When you move them away, show a mood with your facial expression which your partner has to guess. Try several different moods.

But it's not just your facial expression; your posture is also influenced by your mood.

Practise showing different moods through the way in which you stand. Show some of these to the rest of the class. Can they guess what you're trying to convey? Does it work the other way around? Can you change your own mood just by smiling and standing up straight and tall? Try it.

Be an optimist – take control of your mood. Laugh loudly, *now*! Just by physically laughing, you trigger the production of endorphins (brain chemicals that make you feel good).

When you stand up straight with your head up and a smile on your face it is physiologically impossible to be in a bad mood! *Try it.*

Think of three ways to change your mood or that of your neighbour.

Act it out

In a group, imagine that you are a family gathered in the kitchen. It is Monday morning, breakfast time. Act out the typical scene. Then change the mood of each of the characters to see how it changes the scene.

We all respond to each other's moods. Some people always seem to cheer you up. How do they do that? Do you know anyone who brings you down?

Your mood has the power to influence others – bad moods are contagious but good moods are almost irresistible and spread happiness. It doesn't always feel like it, but our moods are influenced by thought. We can choose which thoughts we dwell on, which then will influence our mood. Choose positive thoughts to focus on if you can. (But it's OK to be in a grumpy mood sometimes because it will come and go.)

EXTENSION TASK

Monitor the mood

Create a mood monitor for your bedroom like the continuum on page 165. You could do this using a piece of card and a large paper clip. Assess your mood at the moment and explain why.

Monitor your mood using this device over the period of a week and keep a record of how your mood changes and what influences it.

Mindfulness

Just five minutes practising mindfulness a day can help you become more resilient and clear thinking. Try this:

Sit somewhere comfortable. Focus on your breathing. Breathe in for a count of 7 and out for a count of 11. After a minute or two, become aware of your thoughts coming and going. Don't focus on anything, just see your thoughts as traffic passing through your mind. Notice any tension or stress in your body and consciously relax, working down from your head to your toes. Feel the tension release with each breath. Enjoy the peaceful moment.

Notice your mood after five minutes of this mindfulness practice.

Thoughts create feelings – don't take them too seriously because often overthinking things can be draining!

Lesson 35

Training your brain to wait

 Aim: To understand the link between willpower and metacognition.

All great sporting heroes, successful entrepreneurs or talented musicians *have* to have tremendous willpower. They need it to practise and work hard – even when it hurts, or they are exhausted.

But this willpower also needs to come with metacognition. Whenever you feel like giving up, you need to stand back from thoughts that say, 'You can't do it. This is too hard', and think differently. Successful people do this all the time. It's how they got to where they are.

TASK

How to grow your willpower

What do you want to achieve and what do you need to do to get there? Write down three things which you will commit to doing:

I will …

I will …

I will …

Explain how you will stick to these promises. For example, write them down on a piece of paper which you hide somewhere. For example: I will exercise for 30 minutes 5 times a week. Check your progress every month.

The marshmallow story

(adapted from Daniel Goleman, 1996)

Once upon a time in America there was a group of 5-year-old children who all loved to eat marshmallows. These children were all clever and keen to work hard at school. They all had similar IQs and family backgrounds. One day a researcher decided to conduct an experiment to find out who from this group of children would be most successful later in life. He took them one at a time into a room where there was a table with a plate with a lovely marshmallow on it. The researcher then said:

'You can have the marshmallow now, but if you wait for about ten minutes while I pop out for a cup of coffee, you can have two marshmallows when I get back. You choose. Eat now, or wait until later for more.'

Some children gobbled up the marshmallow straightaway, but others waited for the researcher to return. Those who waited used strategies to distract themselves from temptation. Some sang songs to themselves to keep their minds occupied and others ran around the room or stood facing the wall. When the researcher returned, they enjoyed two marshmallows.

Ten years later, when the children were 15 years old, there was a huge difference between the children who had waited and those who had not. What do you think it was?

Those who had waited scored two grades higher in their tests at school. They were happier and coping better with the demands of school life. After ten more years, when the children were 25 years old, there were even more differences between those who had waited, the Growers, and those who couldn't, the Grabbers. What do you think the differences were at 25?

The Growers had a growth mindset and they were in more successful careers and had more stable relationships. The Grabbers were much more likely to be involved with drugs and alcohol, and to have already been married and divorced. The Growers were able to defer their gratification: that is, to put off an immediate reward for a bigger one in the future. They had developed the habits of growing their willpower so learning would always be easier and they could more easily resist temptation.

Reflection:

What can you learn from this story?

Could anything have changed the outcome?

TASK

Grow or grab?

Write out lists of typical habits of Growers and Grabbers. For example:

Growers	Grabbers
Take time to do it right. *Prepared to save up.*	*Rush through a task.* *Spend any money immediately.*

Now create six strategies for developing your willpower, so you can become more of a Grower.

For example:

- Going to the gym or training with a sports team.
- Opening a savings account.

Create your own virtual reality

Put some relaxing music on and imagine a scene from a big outdoor event playing out on a cinema screen. You can choose to make it a sporting event, a concert or theatre stage or something else.

Really try to imagine all the details. The sun is shining and the atmosphere is buzzing with happiness and excitement. Use all your senses to describe it – the event is big, colourful and noisy. Spend a few moments just watching the crowd and taking it all in.

Then, amazingly and excitedly as you focus on the scene, you realise that the star of the show is you! It's you there, performing brilliantly, wowing the crowd. See and hear yourself. Feel the emotion as you recall the hours of hard work and the pain of reaching this level of performance. Relive the days of practice and the determination you showed. Remember how you learned from mistakes and built your confidence. Visualise yourself being this great success and reflect on the effort that it took to achieve it.

How does this make you feel? What could you do to make success your reality?

For more examples of visualisation exercises see *Grow: Change Your Mindset, Change Your Life*.[2]

---

2 J. Beere, *Grow: Change Your Mindset, Change Your Life – A Practical Guide to Thinking on Purpose* (Carmarthen: Crown House Publishing, 2016).

Mastering your memory

 Aim: To learn how to train your brain to remember and apply this to *all* of your learning.

Revising by reading through notes and cramming makes you think that you are deepening your learning. You may remember more stuff for a short time, but you won't really understand it enough to answer that quirky exam question.

To really remember stuff, you need to *believe* that the stuff you are learning is important, maybe because it is a step towards a long-term goal or because you love it just for its own sake. You also need to be able to connect new knowledge to real-life situations and to stuff that you have learned already. So, when revising, set yourself challenges to explain how your learning relates to everyday things and always try to see how it fits into the big overall picture. This will become your mental model of the world. How rich and complex this model is will depend on how much knowledge you have and how well you have connected it together.

People who learn to *extract the key ideas from new material and organize them into a mental model* and connect that model to prior knowledge show an advantage in learning complex mastery.

Peter Brown et al.[3]

We can only store so much in our memory bank

Cognitive load theory (CLT) shows us that our working memory's capacity is very limited, so we can't remember lots of stuff at once. When our brains become overwhelmed, much of that information is lost.[4] Make your learning more efficient by:

- Recalling and noting what you already know, regularly.

- Breaking problems down into parts. Using partially completed problems and looking at worked examples can really help.

- Using pictures, labelled diagrams and videos, as well as listening to podcasts or audiobooks, on top of your written notes to maximise your working memory.

- Working your brain hard, because the more it is challenged, the more you will remember.

- Talking through your thinking when solving a problem so you get a clear idea of how you work things out.

Making connections to build understanding

Even if you think you've learned something today, it may be forgotten by tomorrow unless you make a special effort to remember it. However, your memory can be amazing. List everything that is in your bedroom. How many phone numbers do you know? Can you remember every name in your class? Think about adverts from the TV – how many can you remember in detail?

Yes, your memory is good but what can you remember about what you have learned in lessons this week?

---

3   Brown, Roediger and McDaniel, *Make It Stick*, p. 6.
4   McGraw-Hill PreK–12, Learning Science 101: Cognitive Load Theory [video] (9 January 2019). Available at: https://www.youtube.com/watch?v=UpA6RdE0aYo.

How to really develop your expertise

We remember by building connections to what we already know. Using quick knowledge quizzes is a great way to review content. Ask yourself five to ten quick questions to test yourself. Have a daily review, a weekly review and a monthly review of what you know so more information goes into long-term memory.

Your memory works by making associations – the greater and stronger the links between things, the better you will be able to remember.

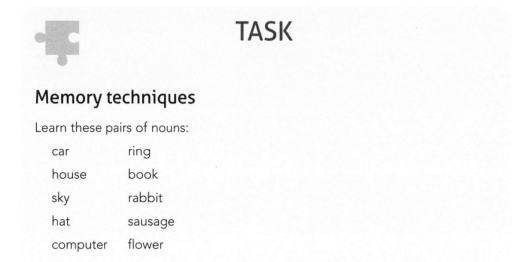

TASK

Memory techniques

Learn these pairs of nouns:

car	ring
house	book
sky	rabbit
hat	sausage
computer	flower

How did you learn them? Did you make mental pictures or use other words to link them together to make sentences. Research shows that the best way to remember is to make wacky mental images. (For example, a car driving through a massive ring.) Rhyming is also a powerful way to help you remember.

Here is a shopping list to memorise:

- ice cream
- carrots
- potatoes
- baked beans
- soap
- chocolate

biscuits

bread

orange juice

pork chops

Take a minute to memorise the list then see how many items you can recall.

Now create a wacky rhyme for each product and a mad image to go with it. How many can you remember now?

 Top tip: Learning names is easy if you use alliteration. For example: Gentle Joe, Saucy Sarah, Perfect Paul or Mad Matthew.

Use mnemonics to help your memory

This means using a pattern of letters, ideas or associations to help you remember something.

For example, you will need this formula in trigonometry:

Sine = Opposite/Hypotenuse

Cosine = Adjacent/Hypotenuse

Tangent = Opposite/Adjacent

The first letters say SOHCAHTOA – which is much easier to remember.

You may find that the spelling of 'necessary' is hard to remember.

But 'Never Eat Cakes, Eat Salad Sandwiches And Remain Young' is easier.

What does 'ROYGBIV' stand for?

Did you know that 'My Very Easy Method Just Speeds Up Naming Planets'?

Make up some of your own mnemonics.

Top tip: Using mental pictures, associations, mnemonics and rhyming techniques are powerful aids to your memory. Advertisers know this. Can any of you remember any TV or radio advertising slogans? Why did you learn them? Did you need to?

Which spellings do you find hard to remember and often get wrong?

What formulae do you need to remember for maths or science?

Now revisit all the tips you have learned this lesson about how to improve your memory and plan strategies to get those tricky words right and remember those formulae.

Curve of forgetting

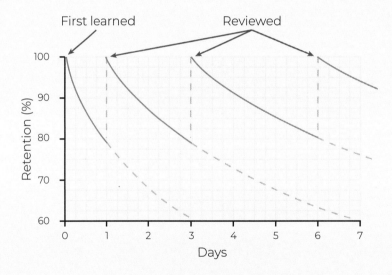

This graph shows how quickly we forget what we have learned.[5] But if we review our learning soon afterwards, and then again and again, we can retain much more

---

5 Adapted from the work of Hermann Ebbinghaus: H. Ebbinghaus, *Memory: A Contribution to Experimental Psychology*, tr. H. A. Ruger and C. E. Bussenius (New York: Teachers College, Columbia University, 1913 [1885]).

of the knowledge. This is very useful for examinations and it gives us great habits for learning.

Regular review is an essential part of learning and memory. If you top up your learning on a regular basis you will find that it stays with you. Look at your lesson notes and add to them there and then. Use pictures, diagrams, colours or other ways of making the notes more interesting and memorable in order to engage your emotional brain. Read them again after a week, a month, three months. Do you remember more each time? Try this out every time you learn something new.

Useful terms

Analytical thinker

Someone who uses higher order thinking to break ideas down into parts or sequences.

Body language

The messages created by facial expression, gestures, posture, positioning and so on, which can have a very powerful effect on communication.

Closed questions

Closed questions are those where the questioner retains control. They ask for a short answer, perhaps only a 'yes' or 'no', or a single piece of information, like a date – for example, 'When did the Vikings live?' instead of 'How did the Vikings live?' See also, *open questions*.

Cognitive flexibility

The ability to think in a different way and manage change effectively.

Cognitive load theory

The understanding that your working memory is limited and can only hold onto a restricted amount of information at any one time.

Community of Enquiry

A group discussion that begins with a stimulus and develops through questions into a philosophical debate, in which everyone takes part and contributes.

Creative thinker

Someone who can generate many different ideas and novel solutions and explores ideas to see where they lead.

Cultural capital

The essential knowledge that children need to prepare them as happy and successful citizens of their community.

Emotional brain

The part of the brain called the limbic system where memories are made and learning is most powerful.

Emotional intelligence

Knowing and understanding yourself well and having ways of thinking that make you self-confident and good at forming positive relationships with others.

Empathy

Being able to see a situation from another person's point of view.

EQ

Stands for emotional quotient (as opposed to intelligence quotient (IQ)). A way to express the measure of how high your emotional intelligence is.

Growth mindset

An attitude of mind that believes that intelligence and personality are not fixed.

Independent learning

Learning for yourself, by yourself.

Internal dialogue

The self-talk that takes place in every person's head as they pursue learning or any other conscious activity.

Interpersonal

The ability to get on well with a wide range of people and to communicate effectively.

Intrapersonal

The ability to know your strengths and weaknesses, believe in yourself and motivate yourself to succeed.

Learning map

A diagram that shows the essential ideas and concepts in a topic in a structured pattern.

Learning to Learn (L2L)

The concept of learning how to learn effectively and transfer learning to a variety of contexts. This would include understanding how learning works for you as an individual and developing flexible approaches to learning.

Life coach

Someone who can support the development of skills for life which can create successful outcomes for individuals.

Limbic system

See *emotional brain*.

Match and mirror

Copy carefully the movements and body language of another.

Metacognition

Standing back from thoughts and feelings and observing their impact. Thinking about thinking.

Mindfulness

Clearing the mind of thoughts to allow focus on this moment.

Mind movies

Pictures and images created in the mind, both constructed from past experience and created from future possibilities.

Mood control

Understanding that moods are a matter of choice that can be controlled and changed using certain strategies.

Mood monitor

A tool for measuring, with a view to taking control of, moods or destructive thinking patterns.

Multisensory learning

The notion that learning takes place through the senses, mainly the visual (sight), auditory (hearing) and kinaesthetic (physical/touch) senses. At different times some people have a stronger preference for learning using one sense, but we all learn with all the senses and the best learning encompasses all three.

Neurons

A name for nerve cells.

NLP

Neuro-linguistic programming – 'the user's manual for the mind'. A philosophy that leads to a set of techniques to help develop the personal flexibility needed for success and happiness.

Open questions

Open questions hand control to the person answering and require consideration to supply a longer answer – for example, 'How do you feel?' See also, *closed questions*.

Optimism cake

The combination of ingredients that will create an optimistic outlook.

P.E.T. brain

The three-part brain: primitive (reptilian), emotional and thinking parts of the brain. Understanding this model can help us understand how and why we experience anger, happiness or any other emotion, and how we can get cleverer. See also, *triune brain*.

Rapport

Elegant communication through body language and speech that achieves a harmony between sender and receiver. Achieved through high levels of empathy and highly developed listening skills.

Self-awareness

Knowing yourself well and being aware of how other people see you.

Self-regulation

Being able to regulate your emotions so that you can respond appropriately in challenging situations and exercise self-discipline when learning.

Socio-emotional skills

The non-cognitive skills related to emotional intelligence, such as empathy, optimism, self-awareness and self-regulation.

Socratic questioning

A form of disciplined questioning that can be used to pursue thought in many directions and for many purposes, including: to explore complex ideas, to get to the truth of things, to open up issues and problems, to uncover assumptions and to analyse concepts.

Thinking brain

The neocortex in the brain, where higher order thinking happens.

Triune brain

Dr Paul MacLean's theory of the three-part brain, used to help students understand how to take control of their learning. See also, *P.E.T. brain*.

Values

Ideals and beliefs that are held by an individual, group or society.

Visualising

Creating and constructing visual images in the mind in a deliberate manner.

Bibliography

Attanasio, O., Blundell, R., Conti, G. and Mason, G. (2018). *Inequality in Socioemotional Skills: A Cross-Cohort Comparison*. IFS Working Paper W18/22 (London: Institute for Fiscal Studies). Available at: https://www.ifs.org.uk/uploads/publications/wps/WP201822.pdf.

Auton, J. (2004). *Education in Human Values* (Horsham: Human Values Foundation).

Beere, J. (2002). *The Key Stage 3 Learning Kit* (Lewes: Connect Publications).

Beere, J. (2016). *Grow: Change Your Mindset, Change Your Life – a Practical Guide to Thinking on Purpose* (Carmarthen: Crown House Publishing).

Bell, N. (1991). *Visualizing and Verbalizing for Language Comprehension and Thinking* (San Luis Obispo, CA: Gander Educational Publishing).

Berger, R. (2003). *An Ethic of Excellence: Building a Culture of Craftsmanship with Students* (Portsmouth, NH: Heinemann).

Berger, R. (2012). Critique and Feedback: The Story of Austin's Butterfly [video] (8 December). Available at: www.youtube.com/watch?v=hqh1MRWZjms.

Berners-Lee, M. (2019). *There Is No Planet B: A Handbook for the Make or Break Years* (Cambridge: Cambridge University Press).

Blakemore, S-J. (2019). *Inventing Ourselves: The Secret Life of the Teenage Brain* (London: Transworld Publishers).

Bosher, M. and Hazlewood, P. (2006). *Nurturing Independent Thinkers: Working with an Alternative Curriculum* (Stafford: Network Educational Press).

Brown, P., Roediger, H. and McDaniel, M. (2014). *Make It Stick: The Science of Successful Learning* (Cambridge, MA: Harvard University Press).

Claxton, G. (1997). *Hare Brain, Tortoise Mind: Why Intelligence Increases When You Think Less* (London: Fourth Estate).

Collins, J. (2001). *Good to Great: Why Some Companies Make the Leap … and Others Don't* (London: Random House Business Books).

Covey, S. (1998). *The 7 Habits of Highly Effective Teenagers* (New York: Simon & Schuster).

Curran, A. (2008). *The Little Book of Big Stuff About the Brain: The True Story of Your Amazing Brain* (Carmarthen: Crown House Publishing).

Davey, S. (2004). *Unforgettable Places to See Before You Die* (London: BBC Books).

de Bono, E. (1985). *Six Thinking Hats* (New York: Little, Brown and Company).

Dehaene, S. (2020). *How We Learn: The New Science of Education and the Brain* (London: Allen Lane).

Dweck, C. (2006). *Mindset: The New Psychology of Success* (New York: Ballantine Books).

Ebbinghaus, H. (1913 [1885]). *Memory: A Contribution to Experimental Psychology*, tr. H. A. Ruger and C. E. Bussenius (New York: Teachers College, Columbia University).

Gardner, H. (1984). *Frames of Mind: The Theory of Multiple Intelligence* (London: Fontana).

Gilbert, I. (2002). *Essential Motivation in the Classroom* (Abingdon: RoutledgeFalmer).

Gilbert, I. (2007). *The Little Book of Thunks: 260 Questions to Make Your Brain Go Ouch!* (Carmarthen: Crown House Publishing).

Gilbert, I. (2017). *The Compleat Thunks Book* (Carmarthen: Independent Thinking Press).

Gladwell, M. (2008). *Outliers: The Story of Success* (London: Allen Lane).

Goleman, D. (1996). *Emotional Intelligence: Why It Can Matter More Than IQ* (London: Bloomsbury).

Gray, A. (2016). The 10 Skills You Need to Thrive in the Fourth Industrial Revolution, *World Economic Forum* (19 January). Available at: https://www.weforum.org/agenda/2016/01/the-10-skills-you-need-to-thrive-in-the-fourth-industrial-revolution/.

Hattie, J. (2012). *Visible Learning for Teachers: Maximizing Impact on Learning* (Abingdon and New York: Routledge).

Kidd, D. (2020). *A Curriculum of Hope: As Rich in Humanity as in Knowledge* (Carmarthen: Independent Thinking Press).

Lear, J. (2019). *The Monkey-Proof Box: Curriculum Design for Building Knowledge, Developing Creative Thinking and Promoting Independence* (Carmarthen: Independent Thinking Press).

Lucas, B. (2001). *Power Up Your Mind: Learn Faster, Work Smarter* (London: Nicholas Brearley Publishing).

MacLean, P. D. (1990). *The Triune Brain in Evolution: Role in Paleocerebral Functions* (New York: Plenum).

McGraw-Hill PreK–12 (2019). Learning Science 101: Cognitive Load Theory [video] (9 January). Available at: https://www.youtube.com/watch?v=UpA6RdE0aYo.

Manning, K., Charbit, R. and Krot, S. (2015). *Invisible Power: Insight Principles at Work* (Lexington, MA: Insight Principles Inc.).

Mannion, J. and McAllister, K. (2020). *Fear is the Mind Killer: Why Learning to Learn Deserves Lesson Time – and How to Make It Work for Your Pupils* (Woodbridge: John Catt Educational).

Merlevede, P. (1997). *7 Steps to Emotional Intelligence* (Carmarthen: Crown House Publishing).

Middlewood, D., Parker, R. and Beere, J. (2005). *Creating a Learning School* (London: Paul Chapman).

Morrish, A. (2016). *The Art of Standing Out: School Transformation, to Greatness and Beyond* (Woodbridge: John Catt Educational).

Neill, M. (2013). *The Inside-Out Revolution: The Only Thing You Need* to Know to Change Your Life Forever (London: Hay House).

Newmark, B. (2019). Why Teach? BENNEWMARK [blog] (10 February). Available at: https://bennewmark. wordpress.com/2019/02/10/why-teach.

Peters, S. (2012). The Chimp Paradox: The Mind Management Programme to Help You Achieve Success, Confidence and Happiness (London: Vermilion).

Queensland Brain Institute (2018). 10 amazing facts about the brain (31 July). Available at: https://qbi.uq.edu. au/10-amazing-facts-about-brain.

Ratcheva, V. S. and Leopold, T. (2019). 5 Things to Know About the Future of Jobs, World Economic Forum (17 September). Available at: https://www. weforum.org/agenda/2018/09/ future-of-jobs-2018-things-to-know/.

Robbins, A. (1992). Awaken the Giant Within: How to Take Immediate Control of Your Mental, Emotional, Physical and Financial Destiny! (New York: Simon & Schuster).

Robertson, I. (1999). Mind Sculpture: Your Brain's Untapped Potential (London: Bantam Press).

Robinson, K. with Aronica, L. (2009). The Element: How Finding Your Passion Changes Everything (London: Penguin).

Rock, D. (2012). Your Brain on Facebook, Harvard Business Review (18 May). Available at: https://hbr. org/2012/05/your-brain-on-facebook.

Rose, C. (2000). Master It Faster: How to Learn Faster, Make Good Decisions and Think Creatively (London: The Industrial Society).

Rose, C. and Nicholl, M. J. (1997). Accelerated Learning for the 21st Century: The Six-Step Plan to Unlock Your Master-Mind (New York: Delacorte Press).

Rowling, J. K. (2008). 'The Fringe Benefits of Failure, and the Importance of Imagination', transcript from The Harvard Gazette (5 June). Available at: https://news.harvard.edu/gazette/ story/2008/06/text-of-j-k-rowling-speech/.

Shakespeare, W. (1998 [1623]). Macbeth (Project Gutenberg edition). Available at: https://www.gutenberg.org/ files/1533/1533-h/1533-h.htm.

Smith, A. (1998). Accelerated Learning in the Classroom: Brain-Based Methods for Accelerating Motivation and Achievement (Stafford: Network Educational Press).

Sorrenti, G., Zölitz, U., Ribeaud, D. and Eisner, M. (2020). The Causal Impact of Socio-Emotional Skills Training on Educational Success. IZA Discussion Paper No. 13087 (March). Available at: https://papers.ssrn.com/sol3/papers. cfm?abstract_id=3562877.

Sperry, R. (1968). Hemisphere Disconnection and Unity in Conscious Awareness, American Psychologist 23: 723–733.

Thompson, J. (2011). Is Nonverbal Communication a Numbers Game?, Psychology Today (30 September). Available at: https://www. psychologytoday.com/intl/blog/ beyond-words/201109/is-nonverbal-communication-numbers-game.

Also by Jackie Beere

978-178135339-4

978-178583011-2

978-178135003-4

Featuring Jackie Beere

978-178135236-6

ındependent thinking press 🏃

www.independentthinkingpress.com